Advance praise for

The *Art* of Diplomacy

"A very original and interesting read about partnership and the important relationship between Canada and the United States. The Heymans model what it means to be progressive in politics."

Former Prime Minister JEAN CHRÉTIEN, bestselling
author of *My Stories, My Times*

"In this insightful and heartfelt recollection of their years in Canada, Bruce and Vicki Heyman give us a behind-the-scenes look at what diplomacy is really about: relationships. In these tumultuous times, *The Art of Diplomacy* is testament to the importance of listening to and learning from our allies."

DAVID AXELROD, former senior advisor to President
Barack Obama, CNN senior political commentator

"The Heymans blew into Ottawa in 2014 in a gust of spring Obama wind and left in the winter of 2017, as the chills of a new era were settling in. Their takes on diplomacy and the ties and tensions between Canada and the United States are as entertaining as they are informative."

BEVERLEY MCLACHLIN, former Chief Justice of Canada

"With their warmth and openness, Bruce and Vicki Heyman laid their path for diplomacy. As you read this book, you will also get to know Bruce and Vicki, and realize that their true belief in tact and diplomacy deserves emulation."

NATIONAL CHIEF PERRY BELLEGARDE and VALERIE BELLEGARDE

"Bruce and Vicki Heyman were highly regarded envoys from the United States to Canada. As ambassador, Bruce Heyman made a powerful contribution in the improvement of the Canada-U.S. relationship. The work he and Vicki undertook in communities across Canada will be favorably remembered by Canadians for years to come. This excellent book recounts significant moments in their Canadian odyssey."

Former Prime Minister BRIAN MULRONEY

"An engaging account of the Heymans' sojourn in and beyond the Canadian capital, and a reminder that both politics and the personal touch matter in diplomacy. Their love of Canada, arts, and the job (which they viewed as a joint assignment) shines through."

CHARLOTTE GRAY, bestselling author of *The Promise of Canada*

"Not only is this book a primer on best practices in international diplomacy, it's equally a lesson on how to keep relationships rich, shared, and alive, whether the relationship is between countries or a husband and a wife."

EDWARD BURTYNSKY, artist and photographer

"Bruce and Vicki Heyman are consummate diplomats. This book is an excellent read and a testament to the people in both countries who work to build the most successful bilateral relationship in the world."

GERALD BUTTS, former Principal Secretary to Prime Minister Trudeau

"The Heymans write beautifully of their time serving our nation as a true ambassadorial team to Canada—which they were in every sense of the word. . . . They share stories of their hands-on and tireless efforts to build bonds of friendship and partnership with our neighbors to the north."

PENNY PRITZKER, former U.S. Secretary of
Commerce, chairman of PSP Partners

"The Heymans' testimony is eloquent. To this day, they remain great advocates for the relationship between our two countries."

MICHAËLLE JEAN, former Governor General of Canada

"A great read. Diplomacy between our two countries is needed now more than ever. The Heymans are an important reminder of how the art of diplomacy and friendship are practiced. A blueprint on protecting shared values and the most important relationship we have."

RICK MERCER, bestselling author of *Final Report*

"In addition to giving us an inside look into a world most of us would never see, this remarkable book lets us look at ourselves in a new way. To paraphrase Robbie Burns, it's a great blessing to see ourselves as others see us, and the Heymans show us just how extraordinary this nation is. In difficult times, this is a refreshing reminder of the great promise of Canada."

NAHEED NENSHI, mayor of Calgary

"I got to know Bruce during his time as ambassador to Canada, and he and Vicki served our country with grace and did a lot of good during their post in Canada. At a time when U.S. diplomacy appears to have gone temporarily out of style, Bruce and Vicki have penned of day in, day out foreign relations and the vital significance of America's relationship with Canada. It's a timely account of the importance of our northern friend, ally, and partner."

AMY KLOBUCHAR, Minnesota's senior U.S. Senator

"A fascinating glimpse into how personal relations in diplomacy can leverage national and common interests . . . The Heymans arrived in Canada as unknown guests but left as great friends of our city, country, and most importantly, our citizens."

JIM WATSON, mayor of Ottawa

"Bruce and Vicki Heyman have given us more than a vivid memoir—they've also reminded us what good diplomacy and politics can be all about."

BOB RAE, former Premier of Ontario, bestselling

author of *What's Happened to Politics?*

"There are no greater defenders of the Canada-U.S. relationship than Vicki and Bruce Heyman. Their stories remind us how we truly are each other's best friends. *The Art of Diplomacy* comes at a critical moment in the relationship and exposes the connective tissue between our two countries in clear and at times surprising ways."

PETER MANSBRIDGE

"This book is like a warm living room in a political world where winter seems to be coming. It reminds us that the fireplace keeps us warm and safe, not fences, walls, or fists."

RUFUS WAINWRIGHT, singer and songwriter, and

JÖRN WEISBRODT, arts administrator

"Vicki and Bruce remind us how to be good neighbors and great friends. They are more than just ambassadors for America, they are an example for the entire world."

SÉAN MCCANN, singer and songwriter

"This book is a gift. . . . It comes from the Heymans' hearts and reflects their core belief that the work of an individual is the work of a couple, is the work of a family, is the work of a community, a country, and beyond."

ERIC FISCHL, artist

The *Art* of Diplomacy

Strengthening the Canada-U.S. Relationship in Times of Uncertainty

Former U.S. Ambassador to Canada

Bruce Heyman & Vicki Heyman

Published by Simon & Schuster

New York   London   Toronto   Sydney   New Delhi

Simon & Schuster Canada
A Division of Simon & Schuster, Inc.
166 King Street East, Suite 300
Toronto, Ontario M5A 1J3

This Simon & Schuster Canada edition April 2019

SIMON & SCHUSTER CANADA and colophon are trademarks of Simon & Schuster, Inc.

For information about special discounts for bulk purchases, please contact
Simon & Schuster Special Sales at 1-800-268-3216
or CustomerService@simonandschuster.ca.

Manufactured in the United States of America

1   3   5   7   9   10   8   6   4   2

Library and Archives Canada Cataloguing in Publication
Heyman, Bruce, 1958–, author
The art of diplomacy : strengthening the Canada-U.S.
relationship in times of uncertainty / Bruce Heyman and Vicki
Heyman.
Issued in print and electronic formats.
ISBN 978-1-982102-67-8 (hardcover).—ISBN 978-1-982102-69-2
(ebook)
1. Heyman, Bruce, 1958–. 2. Heyman, Vicki, 1957–.
3. Ambassadors—United States—Biography. 4. United States—
Foreign relations—Canada. 5. Canada—Foreign relations—United
States. 6. Autobiographies. I. Heyman, Vicki, 1957–, author II. Title.
E901.1.H49A3 2019 327.2092 C2018-906005-0
C2018-906006-9

ISBN 978-1-9821-0267-8
ISBN 978-1-9821-0269-2 (ebook)

To our family—those who provided the path
and those who will lead us forward

The world needs more Canada.

—*President Barack Obama in an address to Canada's Parliament, 2016*

Contents

Part 4

We Are Family, No Matter What

Relationships between countries are no different from relationships between people. They take work and commitment. They are based on honesty and trust. When that trust breaks, the relationship will show the signs of stress. And if those stresses become too grievous, the relationship will suffer. No one wants that.

In relationships, we strive for harmony and peaceful co-existence, even if we are different; even if we disagree. When it comes to international relationships, I can think of few better than the one shared between Canada and the United States of America. I care deeply about that bond. It's very important to me and to so many American citizens. I know, too, that it's a relationship of deep importance to many Canadians.

But before I go any further, I'd like to properly introduce myself. My name is Bruce Heyman. I served as American ambassador to Canada from April 2014 to January 2017.

I also want to introduce my wife and co-author, Vicki Heyman. There's no such thing as a co-ambassador, but if there were, she would have deserved that title and probably many more besides. For three wonderful years, we worked side by side as American political and cultural envoys to the incredible country of Canada, and during those unforgettable years, we grew to love its people, its heritage, its history, its landscape, and, above all, its values. One thing is for certain: Canada—and Canadians—changed us for the better. The experience of living there and learning from its citizens has enriched us in profound ways.

That's all fine and good, you may be thinking, but why write a book about it? And to what end? Let me explain.

We are at a key moment in the history between our two countries. As friends, allies, partners, and neighbors, no two countries have it better than Canada and the United States. We share the world's longest non-militarized border. There is no wall between us—yet—and it is our sincerest hope and belief that there will never be one. We have protected each other through the North American Aerospace Defense Command (NORAD) for six decades. Together, as members of the North Atlantic Treaty Organization (NATO), we have assisted in the safeguarding of Europe. Annual trade between Canada and the United States exceeds U.S. $670 billion. Both of our countries should be tremendously proud to have been part of the world's largest trilateral trade relationship, the North American Free Trade Agreement (NAFTA), and to have negotiated a new trade deal, the United States–Mexico–Canada Agreement (USMCA), which should cement our trade partnership in the future. Through trade, Canada supports millions of U.S. jobs, a fact that I know for certain many Americans sincerely appreciate—although I'm not always certain this message is making its way across the forty-ninth parallel.

As friends and neighbors, our relationship has always been the envy of the world, and rightly so. Canada is—and hopefully always will be—our best friend, reliably by our side throughout times of prosperity but also through war and conflict, economic struggles and political up-heavals. As countries, you can't select your neighbor, but you can select who will be your most trusted friend and ally. Americans have chosen well. We've chosen Canada.

As Americans, we currently have a leader, President Donald Trump, who is systematically poisoning this most important relationship with our closest neighbor. It has taken generations of work and commitment to build such a strong, familial bond, and now that relationship is under stress. It is in peril. Trust and honesty are being eroded through lies and intimidation. The president and his administration are consistently threatening the relationship with our foremost ally while at the same time ignoring other countries that are intent on doing us harm.

During my years as ambassador, the most important lesson I learned about Canada-U.S. relations was this:

We are family, no matter what.

Vicki and I learned this every day, through countless experiences with Canadians from coast to coast to coast.

We learned it when we met with Indigenous peoples in the North who taught us to treat the land—and each other—as sacred.

We learned it when we were welcomed to Canada in two official languages.

We learned it when Prime Minister Justin Trudeau and Sophie Grégoire Trudeau shared with us their dedication to improve the lives of all Canadians and to protect the environment, human rights, and freedoms.

We learned it from the thousands of Canadians who sponsored Syrian refugees and welcomed them into their homes and communities.

We learned it from the people of Gander, Newfoundland, who opened their homes and hearts to thousands of stranded U.S. travelers in the days after 9/11.

We learned it in soup kitchens where we experienced so much kindness and appreciation from newcomers to Canada who had so little.

We learned it from an old fisherman in Peggy's Cove, Nova Scotia, who held colorful starfish in his hands and lamented that they were disappearing from the sea.

We learned it from the tens of thousands of vibrant young Canadians who participated in annual WE Day events, engaging in charitable and community service to help others less fortunate than them.

We learned it when we visited the Peace Arch, a monument on the border between Washington State and British Columbia. "We are children of a common mother" reads the inscription on the American side. The Canadian side reads, "Brethren dwelling together in unity."

Family. We are family no matter what—whether we're north of the border or south of it, and regardless of our differences.

This book is narrated by two voices: mine and Vicki's. Some chapters are told through her perspective, while others are told through mine. This is, after all, a book about relationships and points of view, about respect and roles, and about the personal blending into the political. In some ways, a marriage is not unlike a relationship between two countries. In a marriage, you need to know when to walk side by side, when to lead and when to follow, when to push and when to pull, when to speak and when to listen, when to support and when to challenge. The success of bilateral relations—again, not unlike a marriage—depends upon the delicate dance between partners. It's a dance that requires respect and empathy.

And to carry this further, no two countries are alike. Neither are spouses. As they say, opposites attract. Vicki and I are very different from each other. And yet we shared the same goals as we approached our diplomatic mission: to strengthen the relationship between Canada and the United States, and to contribute to a long-lasting friendship that will withstand the test of time. I made my contribution by working within the realm of politics to promote bilateral trade, to responsibly balance energy needs with environmental sustainability, to enhance the border experience for travelers, and to promote national security across North America. Vicki, meanwhile, made her contribution through her unfailing ability to connect to people on a human level, through culture and the arts, and through building community.

I'm often asked what an ambassador does, and the truth is that each one operates in his or her own way. Vicki and I chose to operate as a couple—"two for one," as then Vice President Joe Biden told the crowd at the U.S. State Department at my swearing-in ceremony. In the end, we decided it would be best for me to accept the official post and for Vicki to do her work in the community. Barack and Michelle Obama knew intimately what it meant to work as a couple toward a shared goal, and in those early days in Chicago, when Vicki and I supported the first Obama presidential campaign we saw—and very much respected— how they both went about their work in different ways but always to the same end.

So here, in my estimation, is what an ambassador does. In essence, the United States ambassador to Canada represents the president of the United States, and, in my case, that was President Obama. I was to protect and promote American interests while acting as a conduit to Washington for any Canadian concerns. I was, in effect, the middleman between two countries. The post entailed a fair share of welcoming visitors, shaking hands, and giving speeches, but it also involved many important files and portfolios, including sensitive communications between the two countries regarding defense, trade, border issues, commerce and foreign affairs, and a variety of geopolitical issues. I was also in charge of seven consulates throughout Canada providing services to Americans, Canadians, and foreign visitors from around the world.

I finished my term of office on January 20, 2017. I had come to think of Canada as my home away from home. Both Vicki and I struggled with leaving and returning to the United States, a country that politically was looking like a very different place from the one we'd left just three years before. I can't help but fondly recall Vicki's final tweets from Ottawa on the day before we were leaving:

At 8:15 p.m.: "Many thanks. We feel such a part of the Ottawa community. It's very hard to say good-bye."

At 8:16: "We are leaving a bit of our hearts with you!"

At 8:20: "#Canada what a spectacular country . . . Thanks for sharing your stories, land, and hearts with us."

Since returning home to the United States, Vicki and I have watched as our forty-fifth president, Donald Trump, has threatened our trade relationship with Canada; as disputes have arisen over steel and aluminum tariffs; as our bilateral relationship has been strained by discriminatory travel bans; and as refugees have fled America and sought safety in Canada because of the current administration's reckless approach to immigration and asylum seekers.

My formal role as ambassador has ended, and yet, in some ways, I feel it is just beginning. It is our duty as citizens to speak up about the importance of strong Canada-U.S. relations and to remind citizens of both our countries about all that we have in common. This book is about relationships. It's a love letter to Canada, our neighbor and best friend. In these pages, Vicki and I have united our voices to speak loudly about our affection for Canada and Canadians. We continue to be very optimistic about the U.S.-Canada relationship. Ordinary citizens have kept this relationship strong for centuries. And no one person has the power to change that.

We want to build bridges, not walls, because as the poet Robert Frost knew well, good fences do *not* make good neighbors. It's time for all of us to come together, take a stand, and work together for unity and positive change.

Let's embark upon this journey, as neighbors, as family, and as good citizens of the world.

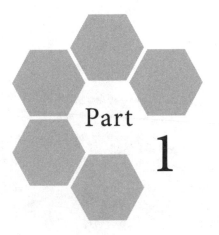

Part 1

Chapter 1

Yes We Can

Vicki

How does a person give?

How do we give as individuals? As communities? As families? As countries? How do we make a contribution and leave the world a better place?

The idea of repairing the world—the Jewish teaching of *tikkun olam*—is an essential part of who I am. It's part of my history and my belief system; it's in my DNA. All human activities are opportunities for *tikkun olam*. No matter who you are—child or adult, businessperson or artist, caregiver or activist—you have the potential to make a lasting, positive impact. And don't we need this now more than ever? Now is the time for all of us to work together to repair the world.

Bruce and I are different in many respects—he's a morning person, I am not; I stew, whereas he compartmentalizes; I love vegetables, while he's a carnivore—but we are most certainly the same when it comes to our community engagement. We feel the same call to action, to giving back. We see this as our duty as citizens. We, like so many others, want to make the world a better place. After all, we're both tremendously fortunate people. We were blessed with good parents. We were born in a country that upholds human rights. We were able to pursue higher education and to enjoy freedoms that are only a dream for many living in less fortunate corners of the world.

It is said that giving is the gift that keeps on giving. When you give back—to your friends, neighbors, community, country—you, too, receive a gift. Your character is strengthened. Your understanding of the world grows, and you become more empathetic. When you give, you're contributing to making the world a place you want to live in. You're advocating for what you believe is important, and you're also working for and with those who may not have a voice or a forum to speak out safely.

In early 2006 I was a forty-nine-year-old mother of three. I was no stranger to philanthropy and community service. As a volunteer, I'd dedicated decades to fund-raising for Ann & Robert H. Lurie Children's Hospital of Chicago. I was appalled that hundreds of thousands of people in my city had no health care coverage, and doubly appalled that many of them were kids. I became keenly aware that we needed a better health care system for our nation.

I worked countless hours raising funds for child advocacy, surgery, a new emergency heliport transport center, and more. I also supported youth education programs in the Chicago area: after-school tutoring, music enrichment for underserved community youth, and university and community college scholarship programs.

My own children were growing up fast. My oldest child, David, was in his third year at Stanford University, and my daughters, Liza and Caroline, were teens with a good sense of direction and purpose. Bruce was thriving in his investment management career and was a partner at the investment banking firm Goldman Sachs. All was well in our world.

This meant I had increasing time to engage in community service.

There was no question of me *not* offering some kind of service. Volunteer work, charitable endeavor, philanthropy—call it what you will—it's what energizes me.

To date, my efforts had been focused at a local level, working in children's health care and education in my Chicago community. The thought of achieving change at the national level or working on a presidential campaign was not in the cards—at least not yet.

As for Bruce, he had philanthropic and political instincts from a very young age, but they were never firmly fixed along party lines. He was drawn to individuals who had a mission; who wanted to make a difference in their communities. When he was twelve years old, he stood on a downtown street corner in his hometown of Dayton, Ohio, handing out pamphlets in support of a Democrat running for Senate. Two years later, at the age of fourteen, he put his support behind President Richard Nixon, who was seeking re-election in 1972, only to be mortified by Nixon's failure to lead with honesty and integrity—two values that are fundamental to Bruce's character. It wasn't until decades later, in 2007, that he took up political work again, working alongside me on Barack Obama's first campaign for president.

Obama's efforts were becoming increasingly known to the community in the late nineties and early two thousands, although we did not know him personally then. Starting in community organizing in Chicago, he went on to become a three-term Illinois state senator. He immersed himself in the neighborhoods, working to help those who needed it most. You don't often see that in politics.

One dinner was about to change the course of our lives in a dramatic way and pull us toward political involvement. It was February 2006, and Barack Obama had been the junior U.S. senator from Illinois for just over a year. Bruce and our son had met him briefly a couple of years earlier in Chicago when he was running for Senate. Obama shook hands that day with about thirty or forty people. In his remarks, he talked about the future of the country and referenced youth specifically. He cared deeply about the younger generation. He wanted to hear their ideas and concerns about the future and make them partners in finding solutions to pressing problems. He delivered his message with honesty and grace. He remembered people's names. He addressed them individually and answered questions directly. Bruce was impressed.

On a February night in 2006, we sat down to dinner with him. It was an intimate party—about ten people. Michelle, Barack told us, was at home with the girls. We listened carefully to everything he had to say. He was just forty-four years old.

Both Bruce and I were drawn to Obama's authenticity. He was smart, inclusive, and his vision for our country aligned with ours. In his eyes, there were no red states or blue states, just the United States. We started talking about a wide range of issues that Americans were facing: affordable health care, the environment, access to education, and equality. After my decades of work with the children's hospital, health care had become very personal for me, and it was clearly important to him as well.

Obama painted a picture where no problem was insurmountable. His ideas were clear, realistic, and practical. He was not part of the establishment—we as a country had experienced two Bush presidents in the White House and were potentially about to have two Clintons. We wanted a fresh voice and style of leadership; someone from a new generation with a vision for what a diverse, inclusive, and equitable America could be.

"We can bring people together to tackle our greatest challenges," he said. And somehow, when he said it, it wasn't idealism—it was concrete and possible. The conversation was so engaging that hours flew by.

After dinner, Bruce and I got into our car, and we just sat there.

"Wow," I said. "He's amazing."

"He has heart and sensitivity and humanity," Bruce said. "He has both emotional intelligence and brainpower. Lots of politicians can stir emotions and rouse a crowd, but this guy is different."

"You know," I said, "Senator Obama should run for president of the United States."

"If he runs, I'm in," Bruce said.

"Me too."

And that's how it began.

Obama declared his intention to run for president in Springfield, Illinois, on February 10, 2007, almost exactly one year after our dinner. Later that evening, he came back to Chicago to celebrate with a small group of friends and supporters, including Bruce and me. We were thrilled. Bruce and I devoted ourselves to his campaign. Many thought his bid was an incredible long shot—he was young, he was African American, he was new to the national political scene, and let's not forget his name, Barack Hussein Obama, which, in America, was a barrier in and of itself. Still, ever since meeting him at dinner, we felt he could win. I remember listening to Michelle Obama as she spoke that evening along with Barack.

"Bruce," I said, "she's as remarkable as he is."

"You're right. She is."

Previous to meeting Michelle, I'd been asked by our friend Phil Murphy, the current governor of New Jersey but then the Democratic National Committee finance chair, to host a breakfast with female leaders to discuss the upcoming presidential campaign. I gathered eighty women—activists, philanthropists, and cultural and business leaders—in our Chicago home and posed this question to them: "All of us in this room have the time, treasure, and talent to engage in changing our country and our government. I'm ready to jump in with both feet—will you join me?"

It was with those words and at that moment that I connected the dots. My political involvement could be an extension of my community engagement and philanthropy. It would be *tikkun olam*. We'd all been working as community leaders, advocating for the causes we believed in—health care, education, the environment, the arts—but to leverage the work we'd been doing as individuals and organizations, we needed a president who would amplify and support this work.

In May 2007 I received a call from a senior member of the Obama team asking if Bruce and I would host a campaign fund-raising event for the senator at our home. When I told Bruce about the request, he looked at me with his head cocked to one side.

"Uh-oh," he said. "Your right eyebrow is arching, and you've got that big smile on your face—the one that means trouble."

That's what happens in a good marriage. You know how to read each other's facial expressions, and you know what your spouse is thinking even before he or she says it out loud. Bruce realized I was determined to do this and that I would not back down, and I knew that he would be in lockstep with me the whole way.

"We're going to do some fund-raising and friend-raising for this campaign," I said.

"Time to fasten our seat belts," he replied, which had the desired effect of encouraging me all the more.

Fund-raising is crucial to the early stages of a presidential campaign. Those funds are used to engage voters and to set a candidate apart from all the others. I had learned a few things about fund-raising through my years of community service in Chicago. One lesson was this: You cannot raise funds by yourself. You need to assemble like-minded people who will draw energy from those around them—energy that will sustain them over the long haul, even when requests for help fall on deaf ears. Another rule is that you cannot ask anyone for anything unless you have given it yourself. You need to have skin in the game.

Bruce and I set phase one of our Obama fund-raising campaign into motion in June 2007. We hosted a garden party at our home that drew one hundred and fifty guests, including Barack and Michelle, a coterie of Secret Service agents, and a few celebrities—one of them being the famed photographer Annie Leibovitz.

Our backyard was absolutely full, and there was Annie taking photographs of everyone. We raised substantial funds through a process I
call the hive model: Bruce and I as co-chairs set a level for donations.
Each couple present was then encouraged to invite other couples to write
similar-sized checks. One honeycomb led to the creation of another and
another, and in time, we had enough to assemble a sizeable hive.

Throughout the lead-up to the election, we helped gather our
community around issues of the day; issues that were fundamental to
Obama's campaign and his vision for America. We canvassed, fund-
raised, and worked the phones. Bruce and I lived and breathed politics
during these days. That first campaign was poetry. It was characterized
by hope for a new and brighter future. Chicago was deeply segregated
at that time—and in many respects, still is today. But during the 2008
campaign, strong coalitions were built across racial and socioeconomic
lines. All of us on Obama's campaign team—women, men, young, old,
rich, poor, black, white, brown, gay, straight—were working hard for
something we believed in. At Obama headquarters, I was surrounded
by people from varied backgrounds who looked so different from me
yet shared so many of my beliefs. Bruce and I bonded with other like-
minded people. We learned from them. We locked arms to change our
country. When you make friends out of an idealistic vision, those friends
are bound to you forever. We called these friends our Obama family, and
the drumbeat of the campaign was "Yes we can."

I remember watching Barack deliver his "A More Perfect Union"
speech in Philadelphia on March 18, 2008, two and a half months into
primary season. It was brave. It was important. It was necessary.

So Bruce and I didn't just write checks and raise funds, we engaged
with voters as phone-bankers and canvassers, trumpeting Obama as the
best candidate, all the way from Illinois to the battleground states of
Pennsylvania and Ohio. Canvassing in the modern era meant knowing
a lot in advance about how a particular street or neighborhood was leaning. Thanks to data mining, campaign workers in the closest field office

With the future President and First Lady at our home during our fund-raiser. Annie Leibovitz was there (*holding the camera, right*) to record the special moment.

We supported Senator Obama for president from day one. We put our heart, soul, and energy into that first campaign in 2008.

knew which households on any given street were leaning Democratic or Republican and which were sitting on the fence. Our job was to talk about the campaign and remind everyone we spoke with—regardless of his or her previous political affiliations—about the issues at hand, about Obama's platform, and the need for Americans to take a stand by voting.

We rallied at a July Fourth parade talking to anyone regardless of political affiliation about Obama's platform and the importance of voting.

We embraced all the traditional and new electoral tactics. We also embraced Obama and everything he stood for. I had the sense in the first campaign that at some level, regardless of the outcome, history was being made. And nothing brought that home more than the first presidential debate held on September 26, 2008, in the Gertrude C. Ford Center for the Performing Arts at the University of Mississippi, in Oxford. I grew up in the South—Ashland, Kentucky—as did my mother. I am very proud of my family's Jewish heritage and painfully aware of the discrimination that Jewish people have faced throughout history. Growing up in the South, I knew that the generations before me encountered signs that forbade "Jews and blacks." Yes, there have been positive changes, but bigotry and racism, both subtle and overt, still characterize many communities in the United States to this day. We have a long way to go before we achieve true unity and equality.

The debate between Barack Obama and his Republican challenger, Arizona Senator John McCain, was at times refined, at other times rough and combative. But the very notion that an African American man would be on a stage in Mississippi vying for *the position of president*—that was incredibly inspiring. I had to pinch myself.

Tension filled the air—not just tension from that moment, but also historical tension. After all, this debate was taking place at the University of Mississippi, still known today as "Ole Miss," a controversial nickname. It is said that slaves used this term for the wife of a plantation owner. And it was in Memphis, Tennessee, just a couple hours north of Ole Miss, that Dr. Martin Luther King Jr. was assassinated forty years earlier, one day after delivering his famous "I've Been to the Mountaintop" speech in which he bravely raised the "issue of injustice" and proclaimed to the world, "We have an opportunity to make America a better nation."

All of these dismal chapters of American history were echoing in my mind as I watched Obama speak that night. He was the antidote. He was the future. He was hope.

Attending the event was a woman from Oxford, Mississippi. "Wow," I said to her, "isn't this an incredible historic moment? I'm so excited to be here witnessing this."

Her mouth was pressed into a tight line. "Oh, yes," she said. "I'm glad the debate is happening here. I'm sure they picked Ole Miss 'cause it's such a beautiful place."

Isn't that the southern way? I thought. I sensed the southern code I knew all too well. Divert. Be nice. Sound harmless even if the underlying message may be quite different. I thought I knew what wasn't being said directly by some at Ole Miss that day: that if you represent the status quo, change is scary, especially when it comes in the form of a person of color running for the highest office in the land.

It made me wonder as I sat there: Had we changed at all? Were we addressing our history? Were we ready to make amends? To move forward? To make a better, more inclusive country for ourselves and for our children?

In the car after the debate, I listened to the pundits on the radio examining the polling of independent voters. Fifty-one percent of those surveyed felt Obama had come out on top of the debate; thirty-eight percent thought McCain had won. Here's what I felt: Obama had won *just by being there.*

On the historic night of November 4, 2008, Barack Hussein Obama was democratically elected the forty-fourth president of the United States. I was in Chicago's sprawling Grant Park that night, with Bruce and our daughter Caroline right beside me. Caroline, then eighteen years old, was filled with hope. We embraced, a hug I will always remember.

"Mom, this is so exciting! I can't believe this is really happening!" she exclaimed.

We were surrounded by friends, co-campaigners, and family. And when I say family, I mean it in a much bigger sense of the word. On that unseasonably warm evening, almost a quarter million people had gathered in the three-hundred-acre park—it spans a mile end to end—to hear Obama's victory speech. I have never seen so many people in one place in my life.

The mood in the city was electric. Strangers were kissing one another, crying, screaming—even the police officers were dancing. Black people and white people were hugging one another, linking arms, celebrating together. It was as if the whole country had united in support of change, equality, and opportunity for all. People were so jubilant, and they were intent on staying up all night. This was the culmination of a dream, a dream that many Americans believed in, a dream that Dr. King had championed but wasn't able to see realized.

People in the park had small TVs and radios, all tuned to election coverage. "If there is anyone out there," said the president elect, "who still doubts that America is a place where all things are possible, who still wonders if the dream of our founders is alive in our time, who still questions the power of our democracy, tonight is your answer."

Sí se puede. Yes we can.

Bruce and I were there as well in Washington, DC, on January 20, 2009, Inauguration Day. The weather was bitterly cold, but still the sun shone on the million or so people who had gathered at the National Mall. We watched as Obama took the oath of office of the president of the United States, his left hand resting on the same Bible that Abraham Lincoln had sworn on in 1861. I remember seeing in the throng a man with a jacket on which he'd written these words:

OBAMA FOR PRESIDENT. DONE.

While I felt a sense of achievement, Bruce and I knew that this was just the beginning. The road ahead for the Obamas would be incredibly demanding. Affordable health care, immigration reform, employment equity—not to mention the challenge of making these reforms at a time

With our daughter Caroline and over two hundred thousand others at Grant Park on November 4, 2008, we watched as Barack Hussein Obama was elected the 44th president of the United States.

when the country was in the throes of a significant economic recession. Within moments, Obama would have to handle the most difficult economic trials that any president had faced since the Great Depression.

What we did not know then was that we'd be called upon four years later to help him with his mission internationally. Our relationship with the Obamas would lead us on a new path that would bring us to a new country—one that Obama would say later the world needed more of.

That country has become dear to us.

That country is Canada.

This jacket says it all. It took an entire community to make it happen. Yes we can.

Chapter 2

Tell Me What You Know About Canada

Bruce

I, Bruce Heyman, am sixty years old as I write this, and I feel robust, healthy, and, yes, happy. I could stand to shed some weight from my middle, but that's a pretty minor complaint. I feel profoundly grateful to have Vicki, the family we've created together, and the career I've had. And I'm not done yet. While I'm no longer the ambassador to Canada, I, like Vicki, am driven to give back. My three years in Canada were in some ways the best three years of my life, and I count my lucky stars that the posting came our way.

One thing is certain: Canada and Canadians changed us. Vicki and I knew only the basics about the country before we went to live there. But living among Canadians, we've gotten to know them well and to respect them deeply. It's changed the way she and I think of ourselves as Americans in the world. It has influenced how we choose to give back, and to whom.

During our time in Canada, we met Canadians from all walks of life, and you know what they all had in common? They were unfailingly kind to us. And yet, here we are, in 2019, amidst a political maelstrom that is pitting country against country, citizen against citizen. Unfortunately, the United States is picking fights with Canada, over trade and other issues. This is not only wrong but also demeaning to our best ally— with whom we share the protection of North America via NORAD and NATO. President Donald Trump is the head bully in this fight. Beginning almost as soon as he took office in 2017, he has disrupted trade negotiations with a number of purposeful non-starters and with the intention of delaying discussions and destroying agreements altogether. He was disruptive, rude, hostile, and inappropriate during the G7 summit held in Quebec in 2018. He has attacked Canada via Twitter and heckled Prime Minister Trudeau. His threats to impose enormous tariffs on vehicles produced in Canada, if executed, would have wreaked havoc on the entire automotive industry—not only in Canada but also in the United States. Trump is threatening economic prosperity in *two* countries, and it has been an affront to Canada. I did not know that I would step down as ambassador only to step back into the limelight to defend our neighbors to the north. But I truly believe it is in America's best interest economically and socially to have a strong, successful relationship with Canada. I also consider stepping up an opportunity to give back to Canadians the way they so kindly gave to me.

But for you to understand that fully, first I have to rewind my story a little to the time when Vicki and I were still deeply ensconced in our American life, in our commitment to help President Obama win re-election.

My father always told me that what made America great wasn't the protection of the majority. What made it great was the fact that minorities could find a place within our nation and have protections under the law. In 2008, when Obama was first elected, we were facing the severest economic crisis in decades. The new president brought together individuals of all ages, races, and backgrounds to work side by side to make the country a better place. Our engagement in his second campaign was propelled by our belief in affordable health care and education, immigration reform, environmental protection, and job creation. These values formed our shared vision for a stronger and better America.

We were eager to be involved in the re-election campaign and proud of what Obama had accomplished in his first term of office. When I was asked to co-chair the Business Advisory Committee, I said yes, and Vicki agreed to be the finance co-chair for the state of Illinois. While her job was to fund-raise within the community and beyond it, my job was to interact with business leaders and discuss the improvements our country had experienced under Obama's leadership, highlighting one of the many reasons he was the right person to lead us for the next four years.

For both of us, the second campaign was hard work but critical to furthering the changes in our country we so believed in. It started in April 2011, with only a few dozen people working at headquarters, but by Election Day 2012, Obama's campaign team at headquarters numbered almost two thousand people, volunteers and staff, all supporting the cause. Vicki recruited a dynamic team to engage a broad community of support for Obama in Chicago and nationally. Together they raised a record-setting amount of money in just eighteen months.

Shortly before Election Day, a senior advisor to the president was in Chicago. We sat with him at campaign headquarters to discuss opportunities within the future administration, in anticipation of a second Obama victory.

"Wow, you've both done a lot of work for the president, and I want you to know we're grateful for that," he said. "We recognize your outstanding leadership in the business and philanthropic communities here in Chicago, and we have been so lucky to have you on our team both in 2008 and now. You've both been tremendous."

They were nice words to hear. Vicki and I had worked extremely hard. In our early years in Chicago, we didn't consider ourselves overtly political people; we were not lifelong Democrats or political activists. But Obama changed all that.

"So I have to ask," the advisor said. "Have you given any thought to what comes next for you and Vicki?"

Vicki turned to look at me, and I turned to look at her. It's not that we hadn't discussed it—but there were so many options and thoughts in our minds, and we wanted to hear a bit more.

"You know that there are ambassadorial roles we're going to need to fill," he went on. "Have you given that any thought?"

"We have," Vicki said. "Most definitely."

Our language always fell back on the word *we* rather than *I* or *me*.

"That's wonderful! I'm so glad to hear it." There was a pause. "So which one of you would like to be considered?"

We went quiet again.

"You do realize that either of you could do the job."

"Oh, yes," I said. "Vicki would be brilliant in the role. She's a natural people person and such a community builder." In fact, many of Vicki's friends were already calling her, urging her to accept a position if one were offered to her.

"And Bruce," Vicki chimed in. "Bruce is co-chair of Obama's Business Advisory Committee. Also, in terms of managerial experience, he runs a highly successful business at Goldman Sachs. He understands trade and economics. I don't think you could find a better candidate."

"I agree with both of you," he said. "You'd each bring important skills to the role if you were to be selected. So who's name do you want to put forward?"

"Both of us," I said.

"Yes, two for one," Vicki replied.

He was taken aback. He looked from Vicki to me to Vicki. "Well, that's not the way it works," he said. "We don't have co-ambassadors. You'd have to work out which of you takes the position."

What he didn't know then was that we already had.

• • •

Vicki and I are both type A personalities. In our relationship, we take turns leading and retreating. If one pushes, the other pulls. I call it "the secret sauce" of our partnership. It's been that way for the forty years we've been together. I don't foresee it changing anytime soon.

We had already talked at length about our post-election options and even what we would do if an ambassadorial role were offered to us.

"I can remember names like a wizard, and I never forget a face, so I should be ambassador," Vicki wisecracked. "Besides, my jokes are funnier than yours."

"Hmm," I said. "That *may* be true, but you do recall that being an ambassador means following rules and protocols, right? Do you really think that's your strong suit?"

No comment, which meant I had her on that one. Vicki is definitely the kind of person who believes some rules are meant to be broken.

We ribbed each other back and forth like this a lot because we've always trusted each other implicitly. What we knew for certain and what we agreed upon instantly was that no matter who held the official title, the actual job would be done by both of us. We would work as a team. We were excited to take on a bold new adventure that would introduce us to a whole new country and its people. By this time, our kids were independent, and their lives had launched. We have always been open to what life has to offer—open to possibility and change.

We knew it was time for us to serve our country in a new way, using our individual skills and leadership styles. We wanted to respond to Barack and Michelle Obama's call to action and do something for our country—in this case, serving abroad. After much discussion, we decided that I would take the lead as the candidate for the ambassador's job. This meant leaving, after more than three decades, a job I loved at Goldman Sachs in Chicago. It also meant that Vicki would stand by me and carve out a role for herself that involved community building through sharing culture and storytelling in whatever new place we found ourselves. This division of roles seemed like a natural fit for us. We were both aligned and excited.

It was time to let Obama's senior advisor off the hook.

"If offered, Bruce will take the job," Vicki said.

"If given the chance, I would be honored to serve the president and my country in this capacity," I added.

There was that look again: from me to Vicki to me. I could tell what he was thinking, but I let Vicki respond.

"To be clear," she said. "There are no concerns here whatsoever."

"Exactly," I echoed. "We agree completely that this is the right option for us. You should know: we're in this together, every step of the way."

He broke out into a wide smile. "I couldn't imagine it any other way."

So it was decided that if asked by the president, I'd serve our country in any posting, with Vicki by my side. But, of course, that was just the first step: there were all kinds of decisions and processes to go through before I was officially given a role. We knew the White House took the nomination process very seriously and that our qualifications and the host country's needs would determine if and where we'd be sent. But every time Vicki and I spun the globe and imagined potential locales, we kept coming back to Canada as a top choice. My job and responsibilities had taken me there for business, and Vicki had roots in the country. Her great-grandparents on her father's side, Samuel and Tybae Simons, had fled religious and economic persecution in Belarus and eventually immigrated to Canada with their six children in 1910 and 1911. They settled in Toronto, where Sam worked as a garment presser. It was a tough existence. They came with nothing other than family, which for them was everything. They lived out their days as Canadian citizens, as did four of their six children and their offspring. This meant that Vicki still had Canadian cousins, like so many other Americans.

We also wanted to go to a country where our partnership would be understood and embraced; where we could truly work together as a team. We knew that Canada was a nation that valued partnerships—after all, this is a country where spouses are called "partners."

Later, when we were asked to name our top three destinations, our answer was definitive and clear:

1. Canada
2. Canada
3. Canada.

This response was deemed unsatisfactory, so we had to revise our list. We added two countries where ambassador roles were likely unavailable.

In March 2013 I received a call from the White House to inform me that after assessing my credentials and passing an extensive background check, President Obama would be nominating me to be the next U.S. ambassador to Canada. So clearly, a few hurdles existed before I would officially be confirmed. Vicki and I were instructed to keep this a secret. Once I was given the all clear, the news of my selection would be announced to the press, with confirmation hearings to follow, ending with induction ceremonies in both Washington and Ottawa. But for now, everything was to be kept quiet.

We were in Chicago when a call came from David Jacobson, the incumbent U.S. ambassador to Canada. He began by talking in superlatives about the job of being the ambassador to America's best friend, neighbor, and biggest trading partner. He was slated to step down later that year. David then shared with me the news that CBC-TV host and political reporter Evan Solomon had three sources confirming that I was to be the next ambassador to Canada. None of the leaks, he assured, was coming from the embassy.

It was a sunny day in Chicago, but a tsunami was rapidly forming around me. I called Vicki at home. "Looks like there's a leak," I said. "The news is spreading."

"Better call your boss," Vicki said. "And fast."

I was making that call to Goldman Sachs New York when Evan Solomon called my Chicago office, and a temp picked up the phone.

"I'm calling to confirm that Bruce Heyman is the next ambassador to Canada," Evan said.

The temp put down the phone and yelled out to the entire office, "I've got this guy on the phone who says Bruce Heyman is the next ambassador to Canada!"

Oh brother, I thought. *Here we go.*

That night, Vicki and I hosted a charity event in our home. It was lovely to see so many friends and people we knew from the community. As things got under way, Evan broke the news of my ambassadorship on his show. It was quickly picked up by the U.S. media. Funny how news travels fast. I found myself a little tongue-tied on more than one occasion that night.

"Bruce, we hear you've been named U.S. ambassador to Canada! Is it true?"

"Vicki, congratulations. When are you heading north?"

The cat was well and truly out of the bag.

Did you know that to become an ambassador, you must first go to school? As I waited for my confirmation, I had to go to Charm School—and so did Vicki. Charm School, as some call it, is part of the State Department. It's located at the Foreign Service Institute in Arlington, Virginia. Think tall, white pillars, cherry trees, a statue of Benjamin Franklin, and manicured grounds with many benches where a soon-to-be ambassador and his dedicated partner can ponder what a long stay north of the border will be like. Here's what Vicki and I both agreed on: we spent about two weeks in Arlington, and there was nothing charming about Charm School.

We spent long days locked in a conference room with a constant stream of intensive, detailed presentations covering every area of foreign service. There was no audio, no video, no slide deck, no discussion—just talk, talk, talk about everything from how to get your dog to your new ambassadorial residence, to national security in your host country. Also, unfortunately, we each had only one day of media training.

Experienced diplomats led the lectures, teaching us rookies the ins and outs of the job. Charm School also included a litany of dos and don'ts—so you can imagine how much Vicki loved that. If you are the spouse of an ambassador, don't ever speak for the U.S. government. If you are using the ambassador's car, the ambassador must be in it. If you are asked a question by the press, say little or nothing. And so on.

Various veterans of the diplomatic corps and their partners shared their experiences. There was a policy team, a culture team, a budget team, a technology team—all brought to Charm School to show us the ropes. Sometimes Vicki and I were taught as a couple; sometimes individually. There were also briefings from "the Canada desk," with technical information on matters such as timber and pipelines. Vicki and I both read a lot. We absorbed what we could, but we realized that everything we learned was from a U.S. perspective. We agreed to enter Canada with open minds and looked forward to learning directly from Canadians.

Let's not forget that our experience of Canada up to that point had been exclusively confined to its cities: Vicki's grandfather's eightieth birthday party in Montreal; my childhood visit there to the World's Fair known as Expo 67; and family trips to Toronto for special birthday and anniversary celebrations. But I did not fully understand the depth of the country's diversity and how progressive Canada was: universal health care, the limitations on guns, the widely held concern for the environment. What I did know about the nation north of us pushed me toward an admiration of its social ideals. I had yet to learn, though, just how conservative Prime Minister Stephen Harper's government was.

Both before and after Charm School, I spent many months making the rounds in Washington. I called the head of every agency I could think of and asked them one simple question: "Can you tell me what you know about Canada?" I met with the Federal Bureau of Investigation and got briefed by the Department of Homeland Security. I met with the Environmental Protection Agency, the Department of Defense, the Department of Commerce, and the Department of Transportation. I asked questions such as:

"How is it possible that an unattended freight train carrying crude oil rolled into the Quebec town of Lac-Mégantic and destroyed half the downtown and killed forty-seven people?"

"What is truth and reconciliation?"

"How many Canadians and Americans cross the border daily, and what are the issues they face there?"

The more I asked, the more I learned. I learned about NORAD and NATO, climate change, pipelines, water, and jet procurements—and much more. Although at the time I was frustrated that the confirmation process was taking so long, I look back now and think how lucky I was for the Canadian education I received in Washington.

I studied and studied, and I waited and waited for my confirmation. But while I waited, there were, fortunately, a few other things to take care of. The State Department thought it would be nice to produce a playful little video to introduce Vicki and me to Canadians. In December she and I went to various Chicago spots on the shoot, including Wrigley Field, home of the Cubs, where the giant electronic marquee announced the new ambassador—except there was a typo. The sign was missing the *b*, so it read:

AM ASSADOR BRUCE HEYMAN

I desperately hoped I'd prove better than that.

Later that day, our videographer took us to Millennium Park for

Chicago saying good-bye to us in style with an "AM ASSADOR" sign at Wrigley Field.

Vicki and I at the skating rink in Millennium Park right before I took a fall that almost put my Senate confirmation hearing on ice.

what was supposed to be a few joyful spins around the ice-skating rink. I was wearing a fur hat, and Vicki was standing at the boards wearing gloves adorned with red maple leaves, holding a cup of hot chocolate. Perfect for Canada, right?

The problem was this: I can't skate. I made it around the rink once, but my second trip was my undoing. I don't remember what happened, but according to Vicki, I hit my head hard. All I recall is waking up in a locker room to blurred vision, a sore head, and no memory of how I got there.

There followed a brain scan at the local hospital, after which I was sent home. I had a whopper of a headache, and, logically, I knew I shouldn't fly, but my confirmation hearing was in Washington that week, and there was no way I was going to miss it.

"Are you really well enough to fly?" Vicki asked.

"Yes," I lied.

"You're in denial," she said.

"I know."

She sighed. "I know I can't stop you. Just don't overdo it."

Needless to say, we got on that plane. When I arrived in Washington, I received a call from my family doctor.

"Bruce," she said, "I hear from the hospital that you had a little mishap on the ice. You need to come in today for some follow-up tests to make sure you're all right."

"Um, doc?" I replied. "That's not going to happen today."

"Why not?"

"Because I'm in Washington."

"You're where?! You're telling me you *flew* to Washington after a major hit to the head?"

"Uh . . . yes, I did. But you see, doc, my Senate confirmation hearing is this week, so . . ."

She sighed. "You do realize you're supposed to be in a dark room doing nothing?"

"Yes, and I promise I'll do exactly that—after my hearing."

"Okay. Just one more thing, Bruce."

"Yes, doc?"

"Good luck."

I took that as a thumbs-up, and I continued on with all the scheduled events for that week. Just prior to my hearing, I endured what are called "murder boards." This is when a soon-to-be ambassador is peppered with questions on any number of issues by a panel of aggressive ersatz reporters and stakeholders. This training was meant to prepare me for my hearing, but it also coached me on how to handle the media scrums and press conferences that I would face in my new role. It was exhilarating. The pressure was on. I had to get it right. It felt like a real test of what I knew, but even more important, it was practice for what I was soon to experience in Canada.

The concussion aside, I felt well prepared. I was ready to answer any questions that might come my way. During the hearing, Senator John McCain asked about the Keystone XL pipeline, which, if approved, would deliver oil from Alberta to refineries in Texas. I told him what I would later tell Canadians: that there was a process under way to address legal, environmental, Indigenous, and geopolitical concerns about the pipeline, and that such a process could not be rushed. The senator didn't seem pleased and walked out of the hearing. Senator Robert Menendez, a New Jersey Democrat and chair of the Senate Foreign Relations Committee, posed a series of questions about the Canada-U.S. border in the Arctic and ongoing disputes about where the border was actually located. I said I considered it a serious issue. Who owns the North Pole and the seabed all around it—with its huge quantities of oil, natural gas, and minerals—was of relevance not only to Canada and the United States but also to Russia and Denmark.

Senator Menendez then said, "If we were to succeed in this process in terms of our claim, would Santa Claus be an American citizen?"

My response was something like this: "As I think you are aware,

NORAD tracks Santa Claus when he takes off. . . . Joint Canadian and U.S. participation will secure Santa Claus's protection. It is my understanding that Santa Claus has a special right as a citizen of the world. He can enter U.S. space without a passport."

The British press caught wind of this and argued later that Mr. Claus was neither American nor Canadian. The overweight, bearded fellow who worked only one day a year and lived on cookies, they declared, was clearly a Brit.

My hearing was complete. I'd cleared yet another important step in the process, and by that time, the post of U.S. ambassador to Canada had fallen vacant. Word was that Republican and Democratic squabbling in the Senate was holding up the final confirmation vote.

Finally, one day in late February 2014, I got a call from Amy Klobuchar, the Democratic senior senator from Minnesota.

"How are you, Mr. Ambassador?" she asked.

"Just fine, Senator. How can I help you?"

"The Canada–United States Inter-Parliamentary Group will be meeting in Ottawa this spring. Will you host us at the ambassador's residence?"

Let me pause here to say that the group, established in 1959, gathers Canadian and American delegates from Parliament and Congress to share information, identify common values, and seek solutions to problems that weigh on both sides of the border. But we had a small problem.

"Senator, I would love to host. But I'm not officially confirmed yet as ambassador to Canada."

"What? That's ridiculous! I'll talk to Senate Majority Leader Harry Reid."

And that was the substance of our conversation. I will spare you all the subsequent phone calls I received to assure me that things were moving along. But as a quick summary, they included more calls from Senator Klobuchar and a call from my Illinois senator, Dick Durbin.

And at long last, on March 12, 2014, almost exactly one year from the original call to inform me of my consideration, Senator Klobuchar phoned to say, "Mr. Ambassador, it's me again. Congratulations. You've been confirmed as the new U.S. ambassador to Canada!"

I was thrilled and greatly relieved. "Thank you, Senator," I said. "I look forward to hosting you in Ottawa."

We didn't waste any more time. On March 26, 2014, at the State Department in Washington, DC, a swearing-in ceremony was held in the historic Benjamin Franklin State Dining Room.

Vice President Joe Biden officiated, and the room, with its cut-glass chandeliers and Corinthian columns, was filled with family, friends, and three former U.S. ambassadors to Canada, as well as the Canadian ambassador to the United States, Gary Doer. Joe was beaming ear to ear at the reception. He announced to those gathered, "Lucky Canada and lucky U.S. With this ambassadorship, we are all getting a twofer."

I read the oath of office. Then Joe Biden and I both signed it.

Afterward, I gave some remarks. Then we celebrated with four hundred guests at the United States Institute of Peace, a strikingly beautiful building designed by Canadian architect Moshe Safdie. Vicki had spent a long time researching and planning an incredible meal that was a delectable blend of Canadian and American cuisines.

But it wasn't over yet. An equivalent ceremony took place in Ottawa on April 8, 2014, in Rideau Hall, the official residence of the Governor General of Canada. There, I presented my letters of credence (formal papers appointing me ambassador) to Governor General David Johnston. What struck me was the formality of the scene: the ballroom with its robin's-egg-blue walls, ornate chandeliers, arched windows, floor-to-ceiling drapes, the Governor General's Foot Guards in their red serge tunics and bearskin hats. But when it came time for tea with Governor General Johnston and his wife at their residence, Sharon Johnston put aside all protocol.

After a long wait to be confirmed, I was sworn in by Vice President Joe Biden as the U.S. ambassador to Canada on March 26, 2014.

"Enough with the formalities," she told Vicki. "Come here, both of you, and sit with us."

We were delighted to relax a bit with both of them.

"So?" she asked. "Welcome to Canada. How does it feel?"

Vicki and I had big smiles on our faces.

"It feels . . . wonderful," we said.

Chapter 3

Home Away from Home

Vicki

Bruce and I arrived in Ottawa, Canada, on March 29, 2014. We were tremendously excited about our new roles, and we were both eager to get organized and get to work. We were also aware of the privilege and responsibility we were taking on. The two of us wanted to be the best team possible and to make a lasting impact. We brought just two suitcases each; all of our other belongings would follow in a moving truck two weeks later.

We were greeted by the chief of protocol of Canada, Angela Bogdan, as soon as we walked off the plane, before being ushered to customs. It was our first time going through diplomatic customs with our brand-new diplomatic passports. Past customs, there were other people to meet—a whole crowd of them, in fact. This group would soon become our embassy team. Everyone was so gracious and welcoming.

Once we were out of the airport, a bulletproof, hulking, black Cadillac was there to meet us.

"Ambassador, madame," a plainclothes Royal Canadian Mounted Police (RCMP) officer from the VIP Unit said. "Welcome to Canada! I'm so pleased to meet you." The VIP Unit provided security not only to the U.S. ambassador but also to the chief justice of the Canadian Supreme Court, and to some visiting foreign dignitaries.

"We're delighted to meet you," I said.

"Are you ready for me to drive you to your new home away from home?"

"We are," Bruce replied. "Just one thing."

"What's that, Mr. Ambassador?"

"I sure hope you know how to get there, because I don't."

We all laughed, and I knew then that we were off to a good start.

On our drive from the airport to our residence, we passed some of the most iconic spaces in Ottawa. We saw the Parliament, the U.S. embassy, the National Gallery of Canada (outside of which loomed the amazing giant sculpture of a spider, called *Maman*), and then past several other foreign embassies, the Department of Foreign Affairs, 24 Sussex Drive (home of the prime minister), and Rideau Hall—all of this within two miles.

Our driver took us to our residence at 500 Lisgar Road, which abuts Sussex Drive and is a few blocks from the prime minister's official residence. We arrived at an enormous black-iron security gate. We were so excited that we got out of the car and took our picture there. Then we got back in and rounded the corner. There it was—the ambassador's residence—a magnificent yellow-and-gray limestone house with a pale-green slate roof, seated grandly in the center of a sprawling ten-acre property.

"Wow, it's . . . tremendous," I said.

"I'm awestruck," Bruce replied. On our right were the sprawling

This was the first time we entered the front gate of Lornado, which was our official residence and home for the next three years.

The residence was beautiful during all seasons, but the long Canadian winters always brought out Lornado's beauty.

gardens, and in front of the house itself were acres of manicured lawn. The residence overlooked the Ottawa River, and as we drove up, I was so pleased to see the American flag flying proudly in front. Needless to say, the house was larger than any we'd ever lived in: thirty-two rooms, including seven bedrooms, three offices, a huge living room and equally huge dining room, a library, a workout room, a pantry, a sun porch, and a rooftop terrace. It was incredible.

As we walked around and familiarized ourselves with the layout, Bruce whispered to me, "What on earth are we going to do with all this space?"

I had been thinking the same thing, but I knew the answer.

"Uh-oh," Bruce said. "You've got that look in your eye again, the one that spells trouble."

Or the one that spells potential, I thought. I knew that with a bit of effort and creativity, this space could be transformed. In fact, I'd spent a lot of time thinking about and planning just that before we even moved in. What if this house were more than a private residence for us over the next three years? What if we opened our doors and invited in Canadians? And Americans? And what better way to make everyone feel welcomed than to showcase the synergy between our two countries by filling this house with great art that represented the best and the brightest artists from Canada and the United States? What if this residence wasn't formal, private, and off-limits to most? What if we created an open-doors gallery; a cultural meeting place where innovative minds could unite and exchange ideas? I looked forward to transforming the house into an artistic and community hub.

Before I could think further, it was time to meet the staff, whom we would soon come to consider our family.

There was Roger, our residence manager, who was the papa of the house. A distinguished, immaculately groomed French Canadian, he had served the house for twenty-five years. "Mr. Ambassador, madame—you'll find I'm very detail oriented, and nothing makes me happier than when an event goes flawlessly or when the house is in perfect order."

There was Jean-François, the effervescent butler: "It is my sincerest pleasure to meet you both. Don't hesitate to call me whenever you need something."

There were Dino and Andrew, our two chefs, who loved food as much as we would come to love them and their delectable—and sometimes spicy—creations.

There were Imelda and Stella: "We serve this house, Mr. Ambassador and madame, and we love to keep it sparkling clean and tidy because it's a historic site."

"Music to my ears!" I said. "It's lovely to meet you both."

There was Miranda, the gardener: "I'm so glad you're here. It's still early in the spring, but just wait a month, and you're going to watch these gardens come into full bloom. The color, the scents, the variety of plant life—I'll tell you right now: you've never seen anything like it. Do you like peonies?"

"She *loves* them," Bruce replied.

And there was Lori, the house secretary. "Welcome to your new home for the next three years," she said before proceeding to relate some of the house's history. "This residence was built in 1908 by Ottawa-based industrialist Warren Soper. He loved the novel *Lorna Doone*, and he nicknamed this property Lornado in honor of the novel."

By the end of our meetings, we were positively in awe of the pride and obvious affection all of the staff had for the history and the legacy of this incredible property.

"Oh, if the walls could talk," Roger quipped. We would come to learn that Roger was both very, very funny and very, very discreet.

"Our goal, Roger," I said, "is to become your favorite ambassadorial couple."

His spine stiffened. "Oh, madame," he replied, "I never pick favorites."

LORNADO FAMILY PHOTO.

Starting at lower left with Jean-François, the effervescent butler, and going clock-
wise: Gillian, my chief of staff; Lori, the house secretary; Bruce; Roger, our residence manager; Dino, the head chef; Imelda and Stella, the housekeepers; and
Andrew, the sous chef.

"Never? Never ever?"

"Never. Ever," Roger said. His chin was lifted high, but there was a playful sparkle in his eyes.

"We'll see about that," I said. This was the beginning of an ongoing joke between Roger and me, and a collegial friendship.

The staff regaled us with stories of the many distinguished Americans and Canadians who'd been guests at Lornado over the years and what each influencer had done there. The list included American presidents and Canadian prime ministers, students, military officers, governors, congressmen, diplomats, bankers, artists, industrialists, and academics. The staff themselves were all Canadian. They were our first introduction to the country, its customs, and its citizens.

Every person who worked in the residence was so lovely and kind, so eager to tell us everything he or she knew about the property. They all took such pride in their work and the residence that, to be honest, I felt we were moving into *their* home. I promised at that moment to always make the caretakers of the residence feel as welcomed and valued as they made Bruce and me feel upon our arrival. Later, I would come to see that this generosity of spirit and welcoming attitude was not limited to the staff. It's a truly national trait, one of the defining characteristics of Canadians from coast to coast to coast.

Our first night in the residence, we slept in our temporary bedroom: the president's room on the second floor. The walls were adorned with paintings of U.S. chief executives, including Abraham Lincoln and James Garfield. On the wall by the foot of the bed were reproductions of painter Gilbert Stuart's portraits of George Washington and Martha Washington—the very first American president and the very first First Lady.

I remember lying there and feeling awestruck. So many thoughts were swirling around in my head as I stared up at the ceiling. "Are we here, Bruce?" I asked. "Are we finally actually here?"

"I don't know what to say, Vicki," he said. "Except that we are. We really are."

I was speechless after that, which rarely happens. We turned off the lights and lay there in the dark, holding hands.

"Good night, George," I said as I snuggled into the covers.

Bruce laughed and kissed my cheek. "Good night, Martha."

Those first few days and weeks made an impact on me. I very much wanted to honor the history of the residence, especially after hearing first-hand how much it meant to the staff and to the many visitors and ambassadors who had either visited or called it home for a time. The residence was then known by the rather dull title of EMR (the Executive Manager's Residence), but Bruce and I decided to give something back to this grand old house, something it had lost long ago: its name. It all started when I shared my intentions with Roger.

Roger got a little sparkle in his eye again. "Madame, that gives me an idea." He went to the garage and brought out a black, circular iron sign with *Lornado* in script.

"Yes!" I said. "That's perfect." I had it repainted, restored, and mounted on one of the limestone pillars at the entrance, just underneath the more formal eagle insignia that announced the property as part of the U.S. embassy.

"What do you think?" I asked Roger once the sign hung proudly.

He looked up at it. His eyes crinkled in that way of his. "Lornado it was then, and Lornado it is today," he said.

The next thing I did to make Lornado more inviting was to update some of the furniture. I didn't want to lose the sense of history, but some of the century-old pieces felt as though they weren't meant to be sat upon or used in a casual way. Up from Chicago came most of our own furniture and china, along with our carefully chosen artwork.

I filled the house with art so that guests would be surrounded by contemporary furnishings and art mixed with a few traditional pieces. I brought in oversized black-and-white photographs of the civil rights movement from the late 1950s and 1960s. In the library on the main

After decades of the official residence being called the Executive Manager's Residence (EMR), we found the old Lornado sign and resurrected its historic nickname.

floor, I hung a large, abstract portrait of President Obama by American artist and portraitist Chuck Close. I would add Canadian art to Lornado later—there would be much more to come.

The first new work of Canadian art we hung was by the photographer Edward Burtynsky. As with much of his work, his photograph *Colorado River Delta #2* invites the viewer to think about our place in the natural world. As Burtynsky has said, "If we destroy nature, we destroy ourselves." I wanted the work of American artists to mingle with Canadian work. I wanted to evoke conversation on topics that matter— artistically, culturally, socially, *and* politically. That meant casting off any sense that the ambassador's residence was a stuffy place. From open doors would lead to open dialogue and communication. Lornado would become a living, animated space where ideas were not only discussed and debated—they were born.

Once you make a human connection, it doesn't matter where you are from. A common language—and shared core values—helped ease us into Canadian society.

Respect others.
I am my brother's keeper.
Gender equality.
Land as a precious resource.

One of the first things we did was invite some fifty journalists— print, radio, and television—from Ottawa, Toronto, and Montreal to Lornado so that we could meet them all. Our instinct was to establish a personal relationship with the press. An open and free press is something we believe in deeply. "What's there to be afraid of?" we reasoned. "If we're open and honest, what can go wrong?"

Looking back, we were a little naïve in those early days. There are cultural differences between Americans and Canadians, many of which we already knew but some that we would come to learn the hard way.

Many Canadians love to talk about—and go on about—the weather. This was a matter of great curiosity to me at the beginning of our tenure. As one Canadian put it, "We see the weather as ours, and we don't appreciate newcomers complaining about it."

Very soon after we arrived in Ottawa, Bruce sent what he thought was an innocuous tweet about the weather—"Snowing in #Ottawa on April 15th? Seriously? #wherearethetulips?"—only to have his comment picked up by *The Huffington Post* with the headline "New U.S. Ambassador to Canada Is Already Complaining About Snow" and the concluding line: "Welcome to Canada, Ambassador. You'd better get a toque."

It wasn't long before there came a knock on his office door at the embassy. The team from public affairs was standing there, with looks ranging from incredulous, to amused, to frustrated.

"Mr. Ambassador," one of them said, "what are you doing on Twitter?!"

The learning curve in those early days was steep. Bruce weathered that little (snow)storm, but there were other, more significant ones yet to come. We ended up taking that reporter's advice. We bought toques— and mittens, boots, and scarves—all of which came in handy on our long walks along the Ottawa River and in the Gatineau Hills.

I must confess that I made my own missteps as well. We were determined to use social media to speak directly to Canadians, so that they could better understand what we valued; what excited and intrigued us. Also, while Ottawa is a major city and the country's capital, it can also feel like a small village where politicians, journalists, and influential people move in the same social circles. We wanted to understand life outside of the bubble. We were eager for feedback from Canadians beyond those closed political circles. Twitter, Instagram, Facebook, and YouTube seemed like great platforms for us to connect with a wide range of Canadians from across the country.

Just a few days after our arrival, Bruce and I went to an arts and crafts fair in the Glebe neighborhood of Ottawa. I purchased a beautiful

handcrafted ring from designer Rachel Rachna Dhawan, who had a jew-
elry line called Brazen Design.

Thrilled with my purchase and eager to share the news of this brilliant Canadian artist, I went to Twitter and sent my first tweet from
Ottawa.

There was just one problem: I tweeted "@BrazenDesigns." I'd added
an *s* to the Twitter handle, thereby unwittingly referencing a porn site
(since taken down) that pitched "panty-less parties."

Our son, David, immediately texted me with an urgent message:
"Mom!! Your tweet!!!!"

A house as big as Lornado is cavernous, and voices carry. Fortunately, it was a Saturday, which meant there were no staff around to hear
my tirade of profanities, the kind that a genteel, cultured woman is not
supposed to utter.

And thank goodness for tech-savvy kids! David got on the phone
with me, and between the two of us and Bruce, we managed to poke
the right options on my screen and quickly delete the offending message. All I could think was: What is the State Department going to
think if *that's* the ambassador's wife's first tweet? We were one of the
first husband-and-wife U.S. ambassador teams to use social media extensively, and we knew it was our responsibility to get it right.

This was among the many new challenges we faced upon our arrival.
As for my own goals, an important one was to establish individual cred-
ibility separate from Bruce. I wanted my own path. I was not going to
play a lesser role behind the scenes. But that meant building my identity
and legitimacy as a cultural emissary. That meant starting from ground
zero. I had to sell myself, make myself a known entity to the community.
How would I engage with the press? What events and programs would I
host to raise the profile of arts and culture within ambassadorial boundaries and beyond them?

I was very careful on my new "perch." I never addressed myself as
co-ambassador. I never spoke in the voice of the U.S. administration. I

would always make that clear up front, whether I was addressing a large audience at the National Gallery or forty people gathered at Lornado for one of the many arts salons we held there. I spoke on what I called "borderless issues": democracy, social justice, human rights, diversity, and inclusion. I said nothing about policy. That was Bruce's bailiwick. I wasn't as constrained by policy. And the fact that I had no official title granted a freedom to work in ways that Bruce couldn't. I was unleashed.

I created a platform for myself across Canada. I forged relationships and connections in the art world on both sides of the border that would lead to dozens of presentations and exchanges and salons at the National Gallery, at Lornado, and at art spaces across the country.

If, for example, I were to bring Canadians and Americans to the National Gallery to talk about their own early experiences of prejudice and social injustice (which I did), I worked hard to fill every seat in the gallery. Every American artist who came north would have art exhibited either at Lornado or at a major Canadian museum, and sometimes both. Bruce's first major speech in Ottawa, in June 2014, was delivered at the National Gallery of Canada. Why? For one simple reason. We were sending a clear message to Canadians, and that message was:

We care about you. And we care about art and culture.

Part

2

Chapter 4

In Bed with an Elephant

Bruce

Despite Canada's great size, in editorial cartoons, it is often depicted as a mouse in bed with an elephant. In an infamous speech to the Washington Press Club in 1969, Prime Minister Pierre Elliott Trudeau said about America, "Living next to you is in some ways like sleeping with an elephant. No matter how friendly and even-tempered is the beast, if I can call it that, one is affected by every twitch and grunt."

How very enlightening this quip is to Americans; how telling about the way Canadians see us. And how telling, too, that as Americans, we are not always aware of our impact.

As Vicki has described, our first impression of Canadians upon arriving in Ottawa in March 2014 was overwhelmingly positive. We were pleasantly surprised and grateful for how well we were treated by everyone, whether it was the staff at Lornado or the Ottawa community at large. And while there were obvious differences we noticed immediately, those tended to be more on the surface level. The word *process*, for example. Americans say *pra*-cess, Canadians say *pro*-cess. Americans say *lew*-tanant, Canadians say *left*-tenant. It's *administration* below the border, *government* above it. No big deal.

But there are other subtle language clues that bely key differences in our national identities. Canadians, for instance, would say to me, "It's cold, eh?" whereas Americans say, "It's cold, right?" Our American phrasing almost demands agreement, whereas that Canadian *eh* allows the possibility of other opinions.

So maybe there's some truth in Trudeau's comment. Maybe we Yanks are a bit elephantine at times—we're definitely big and bold and fiery. We're direct. Canadians are not timid as mice, but they can be subtle. Outwardly, they appear to be very humble and less inclined (than, say, Americans) to be self-congratulatory. But what I learned quite quickly is that Canadians have a deep sense of pride—it's just that it tends to be quieter than the American expression of it.

During those early days in office, I would sometimes meet a Canadian who would say to me, "You're *so* American!" At the time, I thought this was a compliment.

Vicki caught on quicker than I did. There were subtle looks and eye rolls that passed between Canadians when in the midst of us Americans, and being the instinctive person that she is, Vicki understood that right away. "Many Americans think Canadians are nice," she once told me. "But what we don't realize is that many Canadians think we're annoying."

I tried hard not to be an "annoying American" even though I am, by nature, pretty outspoken. I had to learn to moderate that tendency so I didn't offend. The job of ambassador is outward facing. Musicians and actors are used to this. So are politicians. I wasn't coming from any of those professions. I was coming from wealth management, and while I was well versed in politics, having worked on both of Obama's campaigns, my role had been much more about strategic underpinnings than public relations. If someone had said to me then, "We're going to plant you in a place where you'll know no one, and we're going to put you in the public eye," I probably would have said, "Sounds great to me. But you realize I haven't done this before, right?"

There's a lot of learning involved in diplomacy. And mine began the second I became ambassador to Canada. The good part about me taking on a public role is that I'm a people person. I'm social and outgoing. The more people around me, the more energy I get. I'm a classic extrovert. But many things were new to me right from the first day, and first days are interesting—be it your first day of school, your first day in a new city, or your first day at a new job.

One thing I've learned through the years is that to make people feel welcome, the best place to greet them is at your front door. From the outset, Vicki and I wanted to send a clear message to the embassy staff: we're here for you and with you. Our doors are open, so come on in.

Before we arrived at the embassy on our first day, Vicki and I decided to make a pit stop at Tim Hortons. There we stood in line and struck up conversations with the people around us.

"That's a big order you just put in," someone remarked. "Got a hockey game or something?"

"Not exactly," I said.

Vicki then explained who we were and why we'd ordered so much. Soon enough, heads were turning, and people were joining in our conversation, asking questions and making lighthearted jokes.

"Look at that, Americans with Timbits and double-doubles! Oh, your staff is going to love this."

We certainly hoped so.

When we arrived at the embassy, the U.S. Marines were already there at Post 1, guarding the entry as they did every day. They stood and saluted us, which was a different morning ritual from what I was used to, needless to say.

"Good morning!" I called out.

On my first day as ambassador, Vicki and I did what all Canadians do: we waited in line and ordered coffee and Timbits for the entire U.S. embassy from Tim Hortons. We couldn't think of a better way to start off our day!

"Hello, Ambassador Heyman, Mrs. Heyman. Welcome! How are you today?"

"We're doing great!" Vicki said.

"Couldn't be better," I added.

We then moved through security and met a security guard named Bob, who, we would come to learn, was a very special person to the embassy. Appearing a little gruff on the outside, he had a marshmallow heart at his core; he was beloved by his colleagues and incredibly kind and warm, so much so that he dressed up as Santa Claus every year and handed out presents to the children of the embassy staff. Later that year, I would sit on Bob's lap, and he would ask me, "Mr. Ambassador, have you been a good boy this year?"

And, I'd answer, "I've been very good, Bob—er, Santa," as all the kids and staff members gathered there laughed.

But that was yet to come. Vicki introduced herself to Bob as we passed his checkpoint and asked, "Have you worked here long?"

"Sure have, ma'am. I've been here more than a decade. Seen many ambassadors come and go."

"We sure are pleased to meet you, then," I said. "You probably know this place inside out."

"That I do, sir."

"Want a coffee? We have Timbits, too," Vicki said.

He looked at us like we were speaking in tongues.

Eventually he said, "I'd love a coffee and donut. Thank you. And I'm sorry I'm a bit speechless here. It's just that in all my years in this job, I've never had this kind of conversation with an ambassador before."

"Bob, I think you'll find that Vicki and I like coffee and donuts as much as the next guy," I said.

"And we really appreciate all that you do here every day to get people through these doors," Vicki added.

"Thank you," Bob said, still a little in shock.

Next, Vicki and I made our way to the atrium, where we set up our

There were plenty of embassy staff with whom we became friends. One was Bob, a security guard and friend to all. As Santa Claus, he had the honor of asking if everyone had been good or bad and what they wanted for Christmas. Clearly, I'm a big kid at heart.

little Tim Hortons welcome station. Soon staff began to arrive, and we greeted them all personally. We said a few words and declared our intention to get to know everyone. Looking out at those faces, it seemed to me I was seeing a few people in the crowd with similar expressions to Bob's. Maybe they were surprised that this new ambassador "team" had arrived. Maybe they expected us to remain behind the locked doors of the ambassador suite rather than making statements on the ground floor right by the front doors.

After remarks from both of us, there was lots of mingling, with double-doubles and donuts in hand. We had set the tone for the next three years to come.

Daily life as an ambassador was full in many ways—full of new experiences and full of new people. Every day at the embassy, I would have rapid-fire meetings with Canadian and American government officials, business leaders from both sides of the border, and their counterparts from countries all over the world. My workdays were long—often fifteen hours, six days a week—but the work was invigorating. My phone rang early in the morning and late at night. It rang on my day off and it rang when I was on vacation. And I answered those calls. I was, in effect, Mr. Ambassador every minute of the three years Vicki and I spent in Canada.

What was notable right away was just how different the work culture was from what I'd experienced at Goldman Sachs. Goldman was a place with a fairly flat structure overall and a general lack of formality between employees. There, I had been known as Bruce. And I knew everyone else by his or her first name, too. But at the embassy, it was strictly "Mr. Ambassador."

Most days, I liked to walk to work. The embassy was a two-mile (or, as I would come to say, 3.3-kilometer) stroll from Lornado. Here's the thing: most ambassadors arrived at the embassy in an armored vehicle that parked underneath the building. Then the ambassador would take the elevator up to his or her highly secured office suite on the top floor. You may be asking yourself: What's the big deal about entering the building this way? The problem is it meant the ambassador never got to see anybody at the front door, never met anybody coming to the embassy that day, never got a sense of the vibe for visitors who were there for business or to obtain important personal paperwork.

By walking in through the front entrance, I got a very different perspective. Also, it was a pleasant walk, due southwest, with river views much of the way. Sometimes my route took me past 24 Sussex, the boyhood home of Justin Trudeau and then home to Prime Minister Stephen Harper and his wife, Laureen. I would cut across the Governor General's "yard," as I called it, a seventy-nine-acre expanse notable for its beautiful trees—some 10,000, in fact. About 130 of them are commemorative, planted by kings and queens and heads of state to mark the occasion of their visits. My habit was to stroll through this park and read the brass plates to see who had planted what and when. The little oak that President John F. Kennedy planted during his visit in 1961 is now a splendid and mature tree. I also passed other amazing historical landmarks: the British high commissioner's residence—which had been the first home of John A. Macdonald, Canada's first prime minister, from 1867 to 1873 and again from 1878 to 1891—and across from that, the Department of Foreign Affairs. Farther along was the Royal Canadian Mint and, beyond that, the National Gallery.

I was easily identifiable on my morning walk: first, because an RCMP officer walked beside me while another trailed us in an unmarked armored car; and second, because of my headgear on colder days. I was surely the only one on that route wearing a solid-gray flannel Stormy Kromer hat and giant Bose headphones. The Stormy Kromer is a Michigan-made, six-paneled hat dating from 1903, when a Wisconsin train engineer named George "Stormy" Kromer, tired of losing his ball caps to the wind, asked his wife, Ida, to sew him a multi-paneled wool hat that was so snug it would resist gale-force winds.

Over that hat went my noise-canceling headphones, which I prefer over dainty earbuds. Sometimes I listened to music, and sometimes I chatted with my security detail, but mostly I absorbed information through the Hourly News app, which offers major news from *The New York Times*, NPR, CBC, BBC, NBC, ABC, *The Wall Street Journal*, and Fox News. Often my first order of business at the embassy was a press briefing that included respresentatives from various departments. I was mindful of the tendency of bureaucrats to hunker down in their silos, so I did my utmost to enhance communication among all the departments.

Mondays I met with senior staff, and Wednesdays I met with "the country team": a broad selection of embassy staff whom we gathered and included on a call with the U.S. consulates across Canada. I craved discourse and communication and could never get enough of it, and on my way to the office, I sometimes chose to communicate with an honest-to-goodness human being rather than tune into the news. And that human being was often the RCMP officer right by my side.

I was accompanied everywhere I went by two RCMP officers, one by my side and one in a vehicle nearby. There were about thirty or forty in total, rotating shifts and functions. In the early days, we were still getting to know their names and personalities. This one was chatty, that one was shy. This one was from the West Coast; that one was from the East Coast. Our security detail was always on time. If we were driving somewhere, the car was always the perfect temperature when it picked us up. If the security detail was late, it was always for a good reason: the car had hit a wild turkey en route (feathers in the grille were the proof), or it got stuck in a snowy ditch in the Quebec countryside—both of which actually happened to our RCMP companions.

On my walking commute, I always had an RCMP buddy with me. One Saturday morning, early in my ambassadorship, I was with my security RCMP officer Ray. I'd gotten to know him a little bit. Ray took his job very seriously. He was a law-abiding Mountie, and gosh darn it, he was going to keep me safe. He was always on guard and thinking of my safety, even when there wasn't so much as a squirrel in the vicinity to pose a threat.

One calm and dangerless day like all the others, I poked an elbow into his ribs and said, "Ray, how long, exactly, do you think it will take us to walk from the ambassador's residence to the U.S. embassy today?"

"Sorry? Sir, we do this every day."

"Yeah, I know, Ray. So exactly how long do you think it will take us *today*?" I looked at my watch. "So it's eight thirty now. I predict we'll arrive at precisely nine thirteen."

Ray stood there, blinking at me. "Okay, sir," he said.

"So, what I'm proposing is that we have a friendly wager. Which side are you on, Ray? Do you think we're going to arrive *before* nine thirteen or *after*?"

"Sir, I'm not sure that I should be—"

"Oh, c'mon, Ray! Live a little! Are you over nine thirteen or under?"

Ray sighed and looked down at his boots. "Um, I guess I'll say under. I think we'll arrive before that, sir."

"Great! Fantastic. So, I'll wager we'll be over that time. And just to make this fun, because what's a bet without spoils—let's put skin in the game."

"Sir, if you think I'm going to place money in a bet with the ambassador, you've got to be kidding. I could get fired for that!"

He had a point. "Fine. What about this: if I win, I get your RCMP baseball cap." It was blue, with an encircled maple leaf on the front and the words *Courage, Tradition,* and *Esprit de Corps.* "And if you win, Ray, I'll get you an American hat—any hat you want. Deal?"

He looked at me with reluctance. "Sure, if you insist, sir."

Off we went. Now, the truth of the matter is that I actually wanted to let Ray win, but I wasn't about to tell him that. Instead, I decided to simply speed up. I needed to cut a few minutes off our time.

"Ray, why don't we just cross this street right here in the middle?" I asked. It was totally quiet, not a car in sight.

"Uh, no sir. I'm afraid I can't let you do that. Crossing anywhere other than at a crosswalk is against the law, sir. I wouldn't want you to get hurt."

"But it's empty! C'mon, Ray! Live a little."

"I'm afraid I can't allow you to 'live a little,' sir. They're watching us."

"*Who's* watching us?" I asked.

He looked around. Still not a soul in sight. "Um, well, they *are* watching. Usually."

After a few more stops and starts—and a few more times when Ray had to stop me from jaywalking—we made it to the embassy, at which point I looked at my watch. So did Ray. Despite my best attempts to lose, Ray's strict rule-following had made me win.

"Well, sir, I guess that means you're the proud owner of my ball cap."

"No way, Ray. I can't take your hat."

Ray looked down at his boots again. "Good. Because there's no way, sir, that I could give you a used hat right from my head. You're the ambassador. I'll get you a brand-new one."

"Don't be silly! You don't owe me a thing."

The issue of the hat became a running joke between us. A few weeks later, Ray drove me to RCMP headquarters for a meeting with the RCMP commissioner. "Hey, Ray," I said. "How 'bout I tell the commissioner that you owe me a hat?"

"Sir, it's my personal opinion and firm belief that you'd never do that."

He was right, of course, but it sure was fun to pull Ray's leg.

"Thanks for the ride, Ray. See you later."

After the meeting, Ray was waiting for me as always, but this time with a huge grin on his face and a brand-new RCMP hat in his hands, which he'd picked up at the RCMP headquarters gift shop.

"Your victory spoils, sir," he said, handing it to me.

"Ray, thank you. You didn't have to do that."

With my hat that I won as a result of a wager with Ray, my devoted RCMP security officer.

"No, I didn't. But I'm happy to, sir. It'd be an honor if you wore this from time to time."

I treasure that hat to this very day, and every time I wear it, I think of Ray and the many other great officers I had the pleasure to get to know.

I had many early clues that the ambassadorship was going to be more than a walk in the park with Ray or a coffee with Bob. And it goes without saying that while some aspects of the job were great, some were more challenging. Throughout the summer of 2013, while I was still in Chicago, tensions were rising around the Keystone pipeline. The Harper government had rented billboards all over Washington pitching the benefits of the pipeline and urging the United States to sign the deal, while Obama's government was responding to lawsuits launched by environmentalists and massive citizen protests were under way along the proposed route—especially in Nebraska, where local ranchers had concerns about a pipeline going through their property. At the same time, Harper was in some hot water over the issue of a proposed new bridge between Windsor and Detroit, which would replace the function of the Ambassador Bridge. Harper had agreed to pay for the whole bridge—including the U.S. customs plaza—but that wasn't sitting right with many Canadians, who wanted to know why he would ever agree to that.

Shortly after my arrival, even before I was formally presented with my credentials, I was summoned to the Department of Foreign Affairs to meet with Foreign Minister John Baird. He wanted to talk to me and the deputy chief of mission at the U.S. embassy in Ottawa, Rich Sanders, about the bridge and the pipeline. Right away, Baird urged me to get the Obama administration to resolve the Keystone issue.

Fortunately, I'd had many months to do my homework. "There's a formal review and approvals process for Keystone that has been well laid out and publicly communicated," I said. "It's important that we stick to that process. It would also be great if we could resolve outstanding matters privately with each other instead of in the public realm."

That wasn't what Baird was looking to hear. I recall him switching to the bridge issue and asking point-blank, "So you're going to pay for a part of this bridge, right?"

And I replied, "I'm afraid we are not."

I suggested that we might find some creative ways to work out the financials. "This can be a win-win," I said. "Why don't you talk to your people, and I'll talk to mine. Then we can have a follow-up meeting to figure that out."

The meeting never happened.

A few days later, Vicki and I were at Parliament, where we met Stephen Harper and his wife, Laureen, for the first time in his office. Vicki had a lovely chat with Laureen. Then she turned to Harper and explained how she'd recently learned Lornado was the nickname for the ambassador's residence.

"Does your residence also have a nickname?" she asked.

"Twenty-four Sussex," he replied dryly.

And so ended that conversation.

The prime minister then asked me a few questions, but the one I remember most is "Do you skate?"

"Well," I said, "funny you should ask. A few months ago, I hit my head quite hard on the Chicago ice. If American-Canadian relations go south, I can always blame my concussion—and my inability to skate!"

The prime minister did not so much as crack a smile, and all I could think was, "Have I just messed up my very first meeting with Canada's prime minister?"

That night, we were invited to dinner at the Ottawa Convention Centre by Canada 2020, a progressive think tank based in Ottawa. Brian Mulroney, Canada's prime minister from 1984 to 1993, was the main speaker. During his speech, he declared to the press and to a room of hundreds, "We definitely need to see the Keystone XL pipeline

Chatting with Prime Minister Stephen Harper and his wife, Laureen, in the Prime Minister's Office on our first visit to Parliament.

approved. . . . One lesson we have learned from the hassle over Keystone is that we cannot rely exclusively on the United States for any export."

Later in his speech, he called me out directly. "We fully expect, Mr. Ambassador, the pipeline to be approved." This was met by applause. "Now, I know you're not going to approve it, sir, but when you're talking to President Obama, give him my love." I nodded and practiced the art of smiling placidly.

On Good Friday, soon after presenting my credentials to the Governor General, the United States decided to delay the final decision regarding Keystone until after the Nebraska State Supreme Court concluded whether or not the Nebraska governor had the right to approve the pipeline. That evening, Rich Sanders called me at around ten o'clock.

"Mr. Ambassador, we've been summoned at nine tomorrow morning to the Department of Foreign Affairs."

"What? Who are we seeing?"

"Daniel Jean," he replied. John Baird's deputy minister of foreign affairs.

I hung up with Rich and immediately called the State Department. "Has an American ambassador to Canada *ever* been called in like this?" I asked.

"I'm afraid we don't have much precedent for this," I was told. "In fact, I can't think of another time when this has happened to a U.S. ambassador to Canada."

Not good. I talked to Vicki right away. "I don't quite know what's going on, but I might be having the shortest stint ever as U.S. ambassador," I said.

When you're called in to the ministry, you don't have much choice: you go. So off I went the next day, knees knocking.

Daniel Jean and I sat down across from each other in a quiet office. Daniel is a consummate professional and a gentleman. He had his notes prepared.

"So," he said, "you're new. How are things going?"

Before I could answer with anything substantial, he carefully and dutifully read out loud to me the document in his hands, which reiterated the importance of the Keystone XL pipeline to the Canadian government and how urgent the matter was. It was clear to me that Monsieur Jean was following orders.

Once finished, he asked, "Could you please explain American policy as it pertains to the Keystone XL pipeline?"

I told Monsieur Jean what I had been saying publicly all along: that no decision had been made by the U.S. government about the pipeline, that the review process was under way, and that we would await the Nebraska court decision on the matter.

We went back and forth like this—civilly, politely—for a while. Nothing new was being said by him or by me. Next, we covered some other niceties. Finally, I was sent on my way.

In the days that followed, I noticed that all meetings scheduled with various ministers, for one reason or another, were canceled.

Message received: I was frozen out.

On June 2, 2014, I gave my first public speech at the National Gallery of Canada to a group gathered by Canada 2020. In my keynote address, I paid homage to the 150-year-old relationship between Canada and the United States, the two biggest trading partners in the world. The tone was upbeat, even celebratory, as I talked about our four pillars of engagement: trade, energy and the environment, cultural diplomacy, and international affairs.

The audience of about three hundred included Canadian political leaders and dignitaries, businesspeople, some new Canadian friends, and some American friends as well. They'd gathered to hear what had been billed as a friendly chat about the goals of my mission in Canada. After my speech, I sat down onstage for a one-on-one conversation with Frank McKenna, the former premier of New Brunswick, former

Canadian ambassador to the United States, and then, as now, deputy chairman of TD Bank.[1] Our two black leather chairs faced each other, and on the table between us was a bouquet of white and red flowers— they should have been roses, given all the thorny issues Frank raised that night.

First off was the Trans-Pacific Partnership (TPP), a trade agreement proposed between Canada, the United States, Mexico, Australia, and several other countries. McKenna demanded answers to why the American government was taking so long to ratify it. I tried to remind him of the importance of moving carefully and deliberately, but my response was swiftly dismissed. McKenna then moved on to the matter of the Keystone XL pipeline.

"After five years, Keystone XL is not any further ahead. Can you tell us why this project is such a lightning rod in Washington?" he asked.

I reminded my interviewer that the United States buys a tremendous amount of energy from Canada. I explained that we'd received millions of comments for and against the pipeline—comments our government had actually solicited—and that all of this information had to be processed and understood precisely because the issue was so serious for both Canadians and Americans. Listening to all sides was essential before moving forward.

"It looks from our side of the border," McKenna said, "as if you're enjoying the fruits of our economic rents. . . . We don't feel the love. How can we start feeling a little more love?"

"I'll try to start giving you as much love as I can," I said, and the crowd began to laugh and applaud, much to my relief. This was supposed to be a friendly discussion; it was turning out to be anything but.

McKenna outlined another "bothersome issue" and another, until finally I said, "Do you have any *good* issues here you want to talk about? I'm sorry you're all bummed out. We have this incredible relationship!"

"As I'm often reminded by my wife," McKenna quipped, "it might be really good for *you*, but *I've* got some problems."

"Thank God I'm not married to you," I replied.

Laughs, applause.

I was trying to inject a little levity into the evening, to remind Frank and everyone else there to focus on the positive instead of dwelling on the negative. I went on to compare his pessimism to someone who buys a brand-new car and then obsesses about the small scratch on the bumper. In hindsight, I probably shouldn't have said that. I'll admit that in that moment, I was starting to truly understand what it felt like to be Canadian. There had been an abrupt role reversal onstage that night: I was the mouse, not the elephant.

My car analogy proved to be too sensational to leave alone. In the months that followed, reporters and headline writers would revisit my chosen image and use it as evidence of an American diplomat making light of a serious Canadian irritant—specifically, the pipeline. But that is far from what I was doing, and I stand by my overall point, which was missed by some: that Canada and the United States are neighbors by geography but friends and trading allies by choice. This is the choice Americans and Canadians have made for decades. And that should never be taken for granted.

Many months later, I met McKenna at a party, and he talked about how tired and jet-lagged he had been that evening at the National Gallery. He was accounting, perhaps, for his grumpy line of questioning. But looking back, I see that chilly period of time and that night specifically as my initiation into ambassadorship. I was put on the hot seat, and I endured it. I was subjected to a fabulous role reversal, and I endured that, too. I handled the difficult questions—sometimes well, sometimes less well—but I brought the conversation back to what I believed truly mattered.

In late July 2014 a Harper government official approached me in a meeting. "You still like the job? Don't you wish you were back at Goldman Sachs?" he asked.

"Not only do I like the job, I *love* the job," I replied.

A while later, a Harper cabinet minister sought me out at a social event in the Château Laurier hotel. Vicki and I were walking side by side down a hallway when he went nose to nose with me. "We died for you in Afghanistan! We died for you around the world! You should approve Keystone! You should *not* be holding this up!"

I took a deep breath. I smiled placidly. "Would you care to join me inside for a drink?" I said as I pointed to the bar. Apparently, he wasn't thirsty.

Dealing with the ups and downs did get easier over time. As I got to know reporters and ministers individually, I learned the art of diplomatic language. I learned to be less direct. I learned to say, "I hear you, and I will take your concern to Washington."

Rosemary Barton, parliamentary reporter for CBC-TV, the Canadian Broadcasting Corporation, later gave me a "gift" at the Parliamentary Press Gallery Dinner. It was a key glued to a rock—an everlasting reminder (though I hardly needed one) that the Keystone pipeline project was a toe stubber.

The pipeline project was a hurdle in the Canada-U.S. partnership. Pictured here is CBC TV journalist Rosemary Barton's gift to me—a reminder that Keystone was a toe stubber.

Vicki and I often tell people that we experienced two different seasons during our three years in Canada. There were the Stephen Harper months, characterized by an icy chill, and there were the Justin Trudeau months: balmy and warm—as different as winter is from summer. But the truth is that even as we felt the political frost in those first months, we were warmly embraced by so many incredible people in Ottawa.

Governor General David Johnston and his wife, Sharon, and Supreme Court Judge Rosalie Abella and her husband, Irving "Itchie" Abella, were among our first friends in Canada. Rosie, as she calls herself, emailed Vicki to invite us to Passover Seder before we even got to Canada.

We were eager to accept. It wasn't often that we were invited to the home of a Supreme Court justice, never mind one as accomplished as Rosie. She was the first Jewish woman to occupy such a post in Canada.

Chocolate-covered matzo in hand, Vicki and I knocked on the Abellas' door at five o'clock.

The door opened, and there was Rosie, in casual clothes, with a tea towel in her hand. She was clearly right in the middle of cooking dinner.

"Oh, it's so good to see you!" she said. "You're a little early, though. I planned Seder for seven o'clock."

I looked at Vicki, Vicki looked at me.

"Oh, Rosie, we're so sorry," Vicki said. "We clearly got the time wrong. We'll come back in a couple of hours."

"What? Are you kidding? No way. Come on in!"

Rosie and Itchie seated us in comfortable chairs and served us wine in wild, mismatched glasses with stems in the shape of mermaids and bar girls. Their home was filled with Betty Boop images and eye-catching pop art. Anyone who spent time there felt their contagious joy for life. Rosie was like a character from *Alice in Wonderland*, popping up out of nowhere to entertain us and then disappearing into the kitchen to prepare a five-course meal for twenty guests.

"I feel like a kid again in here," Vicki said.

"Me too!" I replied.

We got to know Itchie well, not only that night but also on other occasions. One evening at Lornado, we invited the Abellas to join us as we nailed a mezuzah to the frame of Lornado's front door. The mezuzah is a small, decorative case containing a Hebrew prayer on parchment. Hanging a mezuzah is a Jewish tradition and a way to bless and protect a home.

"Would you say the Hebrew prayer to celebrate this special occasion?" I asked Itchie as we gathered for the ceremony. Itchie is a widely recognized Jewish scholar who has made important contributions to the study of Jewish people in Canada and beyond.

"That would be an honor," he replied.

It was a likely first for Lornado to have a mezuzah on the door, and as all of us looked upon it that evening, tears of joy and gratitude filled our eyes.

In the summer, when I was experiencing the chill in Ottawa, it was Rosie I sat down with to have a heart-to-heart. She helped give me perspective.

"This too shall pass," she said.

I thought about all that Rosie had lived through and all that she had seen as the daughter of Jewish Holocaust survivors. She was born in a displaced persons' camp in Germany soon after the end of World War II. In a commencement speech she once gave at Brandeis University, she said, "It's not what you stand for, it's what you stand up for"—a motto to live by if ever there was one.

She reminded me that while I felt very visible and under attack, I needed to be patient. Time would be my teacher. Canada would provide.

Lornado was starting to feel more like our home. Vicki was well under way with her project of transforming the residence into an artistic hub. The staff felt more and more like family with each passing day. The food prepared for us was always extraordinary, but at the same time, I wanted to experience some of the local restaurants, too.

"Any good Mexican places around here?" I asked my barber one day.

"Yes," he replied. "A place called Ola Cocina, on Barrette Street. It's just a ten-minute walk from here."

"Great," I said. "Thank you." After my haircut, my RCMP officer and I headed over to grab some takeout.

The restaurant was located in a two-story, bright-blue clapboard building. The pale-brown sign over the door promised "fun Mexican food." Inside, the place was small and casual, which was perfect. I was wearing jeans because it was a Saturday, and I was coming from the barbershop rather than from the embassy.

A red-headed woman behind the counter eyed me. "Where you from?" she asked pointedly.

"Rockcliffe," I said, referring to the Lornado neighborhood.

"Oh, so you're one of *those*." A visible sneer appeared on her lips. In Ottawa, the words *tony* and *Rockcliffe* are often paired.

"I'm a Vanier girl," she offered—a way to tell me she was anything but tony. She was from what some considered the rough part of town.

"That's nice!" I said. "I plan on visiting that area soon."

"What the fuck do you do for a living?" she asked.

Gulp. "I'm an ambassador," I said.

"You're not!" Ms. Feisty replied. "Which country?"

"USA," I said.

"You are *so* full of shit, buddy."

"Well," I said, "I may be full of shit, but I'm also the U.S. ambassador to Canada. Now, can I order some tacos, please? And I'll have a side of guacamole and chips, too."

I took out my credit card—and then, for I could not resist—my calling card: the gold-embossed one with the eagle, the stripes, the stars, and the words "Ambassador Bruce A. Heyman," "Embassy," and "United States of America."

She took both and then gasped, "Oh my God! I am *so* sorry. I didn't believe you. Thought you were just pulling a fast one. Will you ever come back to my restaurant?"

"I haven't decided," I said with a smile. "Depends if the food is good."

Indeed, I did come back, many times, because the food wasn't just good—it was spectacular. As I later learned, Madame Donna Chevrier was the name of this swears-like-a-sailor restaurateur. She makes gourmet tacos that are both authentic and adventurous (duck confit and octopus sometimes went into the mix), as well as hot sauces with names such as Gringos Limit and the Release Form, all made in-house.

Not long after that first visit, Vicki and I invited then Liberal Party leader Justin Trudeau and his wife, Sophie Grégoire Trudeau, to dinner at Lornado. I told them about Ola Cocina and how I'd been treated there that first time.

Justin's eyes lit up. "I love Ola Cocina!" he said.

The next time Justin went there, he teased Donna. "I hear you've been roughing up the American ambassador. Go easy on him!"

To be fair, Madame Chevrier definitely made amends. Vicki and I developed a great relationship with her, and we often brought people to her restaurant. When we departed Ottawa, Donna presented us with several bottles of "Heyman Hot Sauce"—with a personally designed label featuring the American and Canadian flags and brewed with special ingredients to be big and bold and fiery.

Was the recipe an homage to her or to us? Yet again, we were finding that underneath it all, Americans and Canadians are a lot alike.

made fresh from our kitche

OLA COC

www.olacocina.ca   62 Barrette

HEYMAN
HOT SAUCE
special
edition

5oz   la merced

Madame Chevrier made us our own Heyman Hot Sauce with in-gredients that were big, bold, and fiery. We never knew if the description was in reference to us, herself, or maybe both.

Chapter **5**

Into the Weeds

Vicki

In Chicago, the first house that Bruce and I lived in had a small garden—just twenty-five by twenty-five feet—but it was packed full of lush plant life. I loved that little garden. There were roses, an espaliered apple tree, and a miniature pond and waterfall. I developed a passion for perennials and a special fondness for peonies, hydrangeas, phlox, black-eyed Susans, delphiniums, purple cone flowers, ferns, and hostas. I would sit out there and listen to the soothing tinkling of the waterfall; I'd watch the patient bees collecting pollen from every flower until their leg sacks were laden and heavy; I'd dig in the dirt and revel in the mossy, mineral scent. Small as it was, that garden was my sanctuary. It connected me to the natural environment. It made me stop and observe the wonder of life all around me. It brought me back to myself.

When Lornado's garden emerged that first spring in 2014, it was floral fireworks, exactly as the head gardener, Miranda, had promised.

Our first spring in 2014, the Lornado garden turned into a floral paradise. There were heirloom peonies, crocuses, tulips, allium, wide-leafed hostas, and plenty of fauna that I hadn't seen in Chicago.

I was awestruck by the heirloom peonies that came up on one whole side of the house; the crocuses and tulips; the tall, flowering allium, with their firework blooms; the sumptuous wide-leafed hostas. I became aware that Lornado, just like that little garden I'd enjoyed so many years earlier, was home to a cornucopia of creatures—and not just flora but also fauna—deer, fox, wild turkeys, hawks, and black squirrels, the latter of which were new to me, because in Chicago we had only brown ones.

"Getting into the weeds" is an expression I use a lot: it means taking a hands-on approach. It means embracing the risk of personal discomfort, of encountering struggle and adversity, of bothering with the details, of doing hard work. And why? Because in the weeds, there's potential for growth. There's something alive that requires tending. There's a garden that may need some attention, but there's no question that it wants to flourish—and it can.

I get into the weeds with every project I take on. That's my nature. That's how I am, and that's how I was with the property at Lornado. Working with Miranda, we set out to make changes and improvements on the garden. A garden is always a work in progress. We put in big hydrangeas and more allium around the flagpole, and floral hanging baskets along the driveway. We put annuals in planters to offer color to quiet corners. I found this rewarding and relaxing. But I didn't want this garden for myself only. I wanted to open it up to the community. I wanted to invite people in to experience what it was like to plant things with their own two hands.

One day in June of that first year, two dozen nine-year-old students from an Ottawa public school came by for a visit. One of the first things we did was go out to the vegetable garden for a bit of digging. The sounds of those children all working together to plant and to explore in the garden was pure magic.

"Hey, look! I found a worm!"

"You sure did," Miranda said to a wide-eyed child. "Let's have a good look."

Getting into the weeds with some local schoolkids. We learned about growing vegetables and healthy eating.

We all gathered round. "Oh, that's a good one," I said. "See how he's wriggling? He misses the earth."

"Should I put him back in the dirt? Do you think he'd like it there?"

"I think he'd like it very much."

We worked outside for a couple of hours. That day, we planted tomatoes, peppers, beans, and lettuce. Miranda taught us how deep to dig, how to gently place the tender new plants in the ground, and just how much water was required. Dino spoke to the group about harvesting and preparing the vegetables. He talked about healthy eating and the job of chef. The children were engaged and excited.

When we were finished, we retired to the grand wood and stone porch with tall, white pillars at the front of the house. The kids assembled around me, and I read the first chapter of Michelle Obama's *American Grown: The Story of the White House Kitchen Garden and Gardens Across America*, a book about the impact of gardening on our overall health and well-being.

A hand shot up once I was done. "Do you know the Obamas?" a student asked.

"Yes, I do," I replied. "When Barack and Michelle Obama first went to the White House, their daughters, Malia and Sasha, were about the same ages as most of you."

I went on to explain that Michelle wanted her family—and all communities—to eat healthy food, and that's what inspired her to inject new life into the White House garden. Michelle's idea was to make gardening and nutritious food accessible to everyone and to engage communities in growing local sustainable food. The aim was to significantly expand the White House garden over time so that fruit and vegetables would be available for the Obama family, for state dinners, and for local food banks.

The garden produced an annual yield of about two thousand pounds of fruit, vegetables, and herbs from fifty varieties of plants—all helped along by pollinator gardens that attracted birds, bees, and butterflies. Finally, Michelle's garden worked hand in hand with a national program aimed at teaching children about gardening, healthy eating, and the importance of physical activity. So when schoolchildren visited the White House, the gardens and the bees were the teachers.

All of these ideas, I thought, were exemplary. Michelle's work brought attention to healthy living and inspired many people to either garden themselves or to promote sustainable agriculture within their communities. I loved her literal grassroots approach, and I started to think more about the gardens at Lornado and how they might be expanded to include more vegetables for our own and others' consumption, with an apiary, which is a collection of bee hives, to do the work of pollination. I pitched the idea to the Office of Management at the U.S. embassy.

After a lot of selling and persuading, they finally said, "Vicki, we like it. It's a good idea." And so we laid out plans for a new, beautifully designed vegetable garden, including a series of rectangular raised beds in which we would grow all manner of produce, including vegetables, strawberries, and even some edible flowers. We talked about the little wooden signs that would identify each of the fifty plant varieties in those beds, and how we would feature the harvest in Lornado's kitchen and make sure that as many guests as possible were able to taste the bounty.

We had a white wooden arbor made and set it on flagstone. On the arbor, we hung an oval sign that read "Le Jardin de Lornado, Est. 2016," complete with a cartoon bee.

And bees were the next step in my plan. A hive is as powerful a symbol as a garden. A hive is a community. Thousands of industrious bees work together to build a thriving hub. And what is the result? Honey.

But like gardens and hives, plans come to fruition slowly, over time, with many hands. They unfurl leaf by leaf. They're built comb by comb.

The Lornado garden was up and running, but it was far from done. I had a plan for other additions. I'd start the apiary once I'd evolved my plan more. I'd bring in hives. And then it was a matter of one more small addition: a hundred thousand bees.

• • •

In 1963, through executive order, John F. Kennedy established Art in Embassies. This program, launched by the president and First Lady Jacqueline Kennedy, saw American art placed in U.S. embassies all around the world to promote American pride and culture through the visual language of art. Art pieces—at times accompanied by their creators—have visited consulates, embassies, and ambassadors' residences in 190 countries since the endeavor first began. Kennedy understood that art could work as cultural diplomacy. The program was immensely successful then and remains so to this day.

I'd already begun to transform Lornado. I'd brought in American art and had it displayed on the walls and in all the formal rooms. But that was just phase one. What I had in mind was to initiate a bold program that took Art in Embassies in a new and exciting direction. I didn't just want a small pathway to the arts. I wanted a highway.

I'd heard it said that history tells us what the world has been, that media tell us what it is, and that the arts imagine what the world can become in the future. My artistic imagination was running wild. What if we brought in artists to be cultural emissaries who would invite conversation and debate on important issues of our time? Of course, government provides one forum in which public discourse can happen, but it's not the only avenue. What if we hosted artists whose work addressed climate change and the environment? What if artists framed discussions of topical issues from their cultural points of view? Could some artists talk about social justice, immigration, and assimilation? Issues facing youth? Health? Thought leadership? Social innovation? I wanted to touch on all of these issues, knowing full well that they come together through art.

I also knew before coming to Ottawa that what I did *not* want to do was align myself exclusively with an individual organization. I had done that extensively in Chicago. Everyone wants a patron, and Ottawa was no exception. The requests poured in. I was determined to work in a more broad and far-reaching way collaborating with many organizations. I did not want to be pigeonholed. Neither did Bruce. I recall well the advice he received from a former ambassador: "Just remember this: you're not the U.S. ambassador to Ottawa, you're the U.S. ambassador to Canada." The Ottawa community was not going to be our only community; we sought out all Canadians.

In April 2014, I went to Toronto for the Hot Docs Canadian International Documentary Festival, where a film called *The Homestretch*—about three homeless teens in Chicago—was set to premiere. I had given a grant to fund this film and was excited to see how it turned out. *The Homestretch* challenged viewers to think deeply about poverty, race, and immigration. The subject matter was near to my heart. For three years, I'd worked with Embarc, an innovative Chicago non-profit that provides experience-based learning opportunities to low-income high school students. These were kids who, through no fault of their own, were experiencing violence, institutionalized racism, poverty, and underfunded education. Embarc's goal was and remains to tear down the barriers to success and to provide youth with tools to help them thrive, achieve their dreams, and contribute to their communities. Seeing a film like *The Homestretch* reminded me not only of how much work America still had to do to achieve true equality in its high schools but also of the many challenges faced by new immigrants and their children.

That got me thinking about my own roots and my great-grandparents Samuel and Tybae Simons, who left Belarus in search of a better life. How strange and fateful that three generations later, I was living in Canada, where they had sought economic opportunity and freedom from religious persecution.

While in Toronto, I visited the Ontario Jewish Archives on Bathurst Street, an organization that houses an enormous collection of documents: letters, photographs, films, and Holocaust memorabilia. I wanted to see if, by any chance, there was a record of Samuel and Tybae. I realized this was like searching for the proverbial needle in a haystack, but

that didn't matter. I wanted to learn more about the earliest Jewish set-
tlers in Canada anyhow, and this was one way to do that.

I told the archive staff what I knew about my ancestors and that my
great-grandfather and grandfather had arrived in the port of Quebec
in 1910.

"Oh, yes," the woman who was helping me said. "Let me see what I
can dig up for you."

A while later, she returned with musty old shipping logs of the Ro-
tenberg Steamship Agency, which kept ledgers of the names of all its
passengers, the ship they arrived on, and the year of arrival. I turned to
the letter S for Simons, and to this day, I can't believe what I found there:
a handwritten entry in the ledger listing Tybae and her five children, one
of them a babe in arms, all aboard the Dominican Line, ship number
141189. My great-grandfather Sam and my grandfather Charlie had arrived a year earlier to set up a life in Toronto, and Tybae had followed
with her five remaining children in the steerage class of a passenger ship

My great-grandmother Tybae Simons started a new life in Toronto
in 1911 with my great-grandfather Sam and their six children.

that went from the United Kingdom to Canada. Even listed was the cost of passage, which for mother and five children was $31.65.

Tears sprung to my eyes. I was speechless. Here I was in Canada, staring into my great-grandmother's eyes through the lens of time. *Look at you*, I thought. *Look at everything you sacrificed, every challenge you faced to help your family and your ancestors have a better life. And look at me, here, now. You arrived as a pauper on this continent. You built a life here against all odds. You faced poverty and discrimination, and yet you succeeded. You did all of it for them, for me—for us. Dear Tybae: thank you.*

One generation was standing on the shoulders of the other. A piece of my family's history had been unearthed—in Canada.

That first trip to Toronto underscored for me the importance of exploring beyond Ottawa and discovering the many treasures Canada had to offer. From our earliest days, Bruce and I made an effort to see the country and to meet its people. We wanted to understand Canadians, and we wanted Canadians to understand us as well.

In hindsight, the Harper government's chilly reception was a great accelerator, for it helped push us out on the road not once but twice in 2014. As Bruce and I traveled, sometimes together, sometimes separately, we connected with Canadians all across the country. The two of us visited each of the seven consulates (in Vancouver, Calgary, Winnipeg, Toronto, Montreal, Quebec City, and Halifax), and we met all the consuls general and State Department staff representing the U.S. mission in Canada. Our first trip took us to seven provinces and fifteen cities in twenty-one days. We met every premier, nearly every lieutenant governor, as many cultural leaders as we possibly could, and just about every mayor of every major city. We also met artists and artisans of all varieties.

Whenever you meet a true artisan and develop a relationship—even if only for a short while—you form a bond by experiencing his or her craft. Such was the case when we met Johnny Flynn, who runs his own oyster farm on Colville Bay, Prince Edward Island. He took us to the water's edge, where he explained his process for growing and harvesting oysters.

"The dories go out at dawn, and fishermen use twelve-foot-long tongs to haul in the oysters," he said. He passed us one of the odd tools, which looked like two large rakes fastened together.

"Wow," I said. "Those would toss a really big salad."

Johnny laughed. "Here, see this?" He brought us a bucket with a fresh harvest of gorgeous oysters, which he dumped onto a metal counter. Johnny's oysters were covered with distinctive green algae that I'd never seen before.

"Do you think the algae is the key to the flavor?" I asked.

"Maybe," Johnny said. "I'll tell you one thing, though. Our oysters are more delicious than other oysters. Would you like to try them?"

"Of course!"

Johnny then picked up an oyster from the counter and proceeded to shuck it right there with his oyster knife. All my life I had eaten oysters in restaurants, prepared perfectly on a bed of ice, served with sauces, a side of lemon, and delicate little forks.

Once the oyster was shucked, Johnny handed it to me. "Just like that?" I asked.

"Of course!" he said. "Just grab it and suck it back."

Bruce and I both did so, and I can tell you that the taste was like nothing else. How sweet they were, and plump and fresh and salty, too. It was the taste of all the goodness of the ocean in one little shell.

"Incredible, isn't it?" Johnny said. "That's the taste of my home."

After that, whenever we ordered oysters in Canada, we always asked, "Do you have any of Johnny's from Colville Bay?" And whenever a restaurant did, we'd message Johnny and say, "Johnny! We're eating your oysters, and it's the taste of your home!"

No matter what place we visited, Bruce and I almost always tried the

Bruce and I enjoyed traveling around Canada and meeting everyone from activists to artisans. In PEI, we met Johnny, owner of Colville Bay Oyster Company,
who harvests the tastiest of oysters.

food and drink that was put before us. With one exception: the Sourtoe
Cocktail served to Bruce in Dawson City in the Yukon. As he learned, in
the 1920s, somewhere nearby, two rum-running brothers named Louie
and Otto Linken were caught in a blizzard while on a dogsled run. Louie's foot at some point went right through the icy lake they were navigating and into the frigid water. Eventually they reached the safety of their
cabin, but Louie's frostbitten toe could not be saved. He fortified himself
with rum before Otto severed it with an axe.

In 1973 a river barge pilot named Captain Dick Stevenson was clean-
ing the old Linken brothers' cabin and found the toe in a jar of alcohol.
He then concocted the Sourtoe Cocktail: made out of one ounce of any
powerful liquor and a very black, dehydrated human toe.

To be a member of Stevenson's elite Sourtoe Cocktail Club, one must drink a whole Sourtoe Cocktail. More than one hundred thousand people from all over the world have joined the club. In some preparations of the cocktail, the toe is wrung a little so that the juices are dripped into the glass.

As they say in Dawson City, "You can drink it fast, you can drink it slow, but your lips have gotta touch the toe."

There is a fine for swallowing the toe. It used to be $500. Incredibly, several individuals have had to pay the fine, one as recently as 2013, so the "deterrent" fine has been jacked up to $2,500. In total, ten black toes have been donated to the "cause," so this quintessentially Canadian tradition endures despite the best efforts of the swallowers.

Something about that toe being squeezed in front of him really turned Bruce off. He was offered the cocktail more than once, but he never did try it.

"I couldn't do it, Vicki," he once said. "That is one line I just can't toe."

Eye roll. My jokes are definitely better than his.

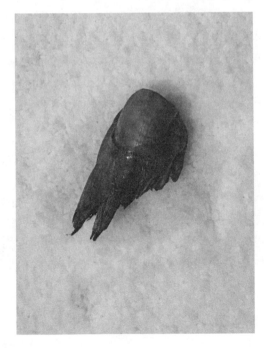

Wherever we traveled, we tried the food, but Bruce and I drew the line at the Sourtoe Cocktail, made of one ounce of liquor and a very black human toe. You see the toe awaiting its next customer here.

Our education in northern cuisine constituted a hallmark of our time in Canada. I did not know about shore lunches until we enjoyed one atop a rocky outcrop on Great Slave Lake. This was a picnic unlike any Bruce and I had ever experienced. Bob McLeod, the premier of the Northwest Territories, along with three members of his cabinet, picked us up in Yellowknife in a motorboat. He proceeded to show us the lake and the rolling hills surrounding it, and was more or less giving us the grand tour from the water when he said suddenly, "Shall we stop for lunch?"

Bruce and I were puzzled. There was definitely no restaurant in sight; no picnic basket, either. Bob gently docked the boat on that rugged coastline.

"What's going on?" I asked Bruce quietly.

"I have no idea," he said. "Which means it's going to be great."

Out came a blackened grill and frying pan. A fire was made in a circle of stones, and a mixed vegetable salad was tossed and lemon wedges cut while a young member of our entourage walked to the edge of a high outcrop, fishing rod in hand, and dropped his line in the water. In what seemed like no time, he had caught our lunch.

When only minutes transpire in this sequence—the fish are caught, and then gutted and cleaned onshore before being dropped into a frying pan with butter and lemon over a wood fire—that's called "a shore lunch." Each plate of fish and salad was adorned with wild cornflowers (also called "bachelor's buttons") that were royal purple or pale pink or white. As far as lunches go, this was as fresh and as perfect as they come.

From Yellowknife, we took a very small plane seven hundred miles farther north to Tuktoyaktuk, a small community on the edge of the Arctic Sea. Also aboard were Peter Kujawinski, consul general in Calgary; an RCMP officer; and an older gentleman who was traveling to Tuk for fishing. We learned that the name Tuktoyaktuk is actually an anglicized version of the word *Tuktuyaaqtuuq*, from the Inuvialuktun language. It means "resembling a caribou."

"Why is it called that?" I asked the older man.

"That's an old legend. Goes way back. There was once a woman in the village who observed caribou wade into the ocean and turn into stone. So that's where the name comes from."

Halfway to Tuk, our fisherman hitchhiker declared to our pilot his need for a washroom. Our plane most certainly did not have one.

"Okay, no problem," the pilot said. "We'll make a pit stop."

When I looked out the window, all I could see were trees and lakes far into the distance.

"Bruce, do you see a runway down there?"

"No, Vicki, I do not see a runway down there."

"So . . ."

"I have no idea. But that means it's going to be great."

Amazingly, our pilot approached the treetops, and into our view came a dirt runway in the middle of the forest. We made our brief pit stop, Northwest Territories style.

Back in the air, approaching Tuktoyaktuk, the pilot said the one thing you never want to hear a pilot say: "Uh-oh."

Bruce leaned forward and asked, "Is there a problem?"

"No wind," he said.

"And why is that a problem?"

"You'll see," the pilot replied mysteriously.

We landed smoothly, much to my relief, and everything seemed fine. But when we exited the plane, we were swarmed by more black flies than I thought existed on the planet. Now I understood why the pilot had wanted wind. Fortunately, we were also greeted by much friendlier beings: Darrel Nasogaluak, the mayor of the hamlet, who conveniently doubles as Tuk's air traffic controller, and Eileen Jacobson, born and raised in town.

"Darrel, Eileen, we're so thrilled to be here. Thank you so much for taking the time to meet with us," I said.

Bruce handed them a big box of Tim Hortons donuts that we'd brought for them.

"Oh, you don't know what a treat this is for us up here!" Darrel enthused. "I don't think you could have brought us anything better!"

"You're coming to my place for lunch," Eileen announced happily, so the two of us piled into her truck for the short drive to her house. Outside was a yurt, with dozens of fur pelts hanging on racks. Eileen's husband, Billy, was there to greet us.

"Hello!" He beamed. "We're happy you're here!" I'm not sure what was more amazing to me: his incredibly warm welcome, as if he'd known us for years, or his polar bear pants. These were a shocking sight for us, though we knew that the people of the North had sustainably and respectfully hunted polar bear and many other animals for thousands of years.

Inside, set out on Eileen's kitchen table, were muktuk (the skin and blubber of a whale, diced and served raw), caribou stew, and smoked fish. All of these dishes were like nothing we had ever tasted before, and we thanked Eileen for giving us this new and wonderful experience.

"Very happy to have you here," she said. "We don't get all that many American visitors from Ottawa."

Bruce and I were fascinated with the town and the culture of the Far North, and we peppered Eileen with questions. Later, she said, "I want to show you something. Let's go."

So off we went in her gray truck. Eileen took us to a cavernous space set deep below the permafrost. This was the community freezer. Steps led to a door with a sturdy lock meant to keep out four-legged pilferers.

"Wow! Let's go in," Bruce said.

The RCMP security detail had other ideas. "Ambassador, I can't let you descend into a freezing-cold meat cooler."

Bruce relented. In truth, we were happy just to see the freezer and to spend some time with the warm and accommodating villagers who wanted to share with us their way of life. Wherever we went in the North, we were greeted by people who were amazingly hospitable and eager to educate

In Tuktoyaktuk, a remote village in northern Canada, with Eileen Jacobson, our guide and host. To her left hangs her smoked fish, which was unlike anything we'd ever tried before.

Eileen also showed us the community freezer, where the whole village kept their food preserved and away from four-legged thieves.

us about their traditions and also about their fears of a vanishing way of life. At Great Bear Lake, one of the largest lakes in the world, we visited the only human settlement on the lake: the village of Déline (population five hundred). *Déline* means "where the waters flow"—a reference to the head-waters of the Great Bear River. The people are mostly Sahtuto'ine—the Bear Lake People—and they speak the North Slavey language.

Bruce and I were ushered to a modest community center, where we were introduced to a chief, a deputy chief, and two male elders, both appearing to be well into their nineties. The two elders spoke North Slavey very deliberately, in a low tone of voice. The chief and the deputy clearly admired them and treated them with the utmost respect. The bilingual chief acted as translator between the elders and us.

"They want to welcome you to the home of the Bear Lake People," the chief said. "They are happy you came to visit them and want to tell you more about our culture."

"Please tell them that we, too, are deeply honored to be here," I said.

"And tell them we are here to listen and learn," Bruce added.

Our words were translated. The elders nodded. Then each elder clasped his hands as he spoke with great dignity and cadence, and those words were translated to us.

"We are the stewards of this great lake and the land around it," said one. "Both have to be protected for future generations."

I could feel goose bumps rising on my arms.

"One of our elders, Eht'se Ayah, he was a prophet. He was born in 1857, and he died in 1940 at age eighty-three. He was able to see through time. Some of our people—they can do that. They can see to the past, and they can see to the future. When he was alive, people would come from all over the Arctic to hear him speak. Do you know what he said?"

We did not.

"He said that one day people from the South would come to Great Bear Lake. He said they would come here because it would be one of the few places left on earth with clean water to drink and fresh fish to eat.

When they come, Great Bear Lake will be packed full of boats, and at that moment, our people will have a decision to make. We will have to decide how we will help. Eht'se Ayah said that people have survived for thousands of years by sticking together, and the only way we'll last is by continuing to do so.

"His prophecy hasn't come true yet, but we believe it will. We believe the earth is not being respected. And we see people who don't understand that the land, the animals, water, each other—this is all we have. Our lake—Great Bear Lake—it's not like other lakes. Do you understand what we're saying? Our lake is critical to the survival of humankind."

They spoke with such solemnity and intensity. We could see the story in their eyes and felt it delivered straight to our hearts.

I looked over at Bruce. He's not prone to emotional demonstrations, so I knew when I saw tears in his eyes that the elders' words had shaken him to the core, as they had me. These people had lived, survived, suffered, and thrived in the North for more than two thousand years. They were the stewards of that immense body of water, and they were the stewards of the land. Bruce and I felt in that moment that they were articulating and prophesizing exactly what all the greatest scientific minds from the Western world were also articulating and prophesizing: that climate change is real and that if we don't do something soon to stop it, it might be too late.

The expression of that prophecy was one of the most powerful things that Bruce and I have ever experienced. That moment galvanized us to do more and speak more about the impact of climate change and the importance of preserving water across the entire globe—before we run out.

We left that small office visibly moved and deeply appreciative. We were later taken to the shrine of Eht'se Ayah. Surrounded by candles, statues of Jesus and the Virgin Mary, flowers, and an open Bible was the framed black-and-white photograph of a bearded man in what looked like a bearskin hat. There were also images of him in his youth. The fresh flowers on the shrine were testament that Eht'se Ayah and his prophesies have not been forgotten. I thought about how North Americans—Americans and Canadians—so often look to the Far East for spiritual guidance. And yet it was all right there; all the guidance we needed, right on our own continent. *May our elders*, I thought, *be remembered always.*

We traveled widely that first year, east and west, and from coast to coast to coast, but whenever the compass pointed north (and sometimes not even that far north), something extraordinary happened. We visited Kenauk in Quebec and enjoyed catching and releasing fish after fish in the surrounding waters. We enjoyed Canadian cottage life, sitting in Muskoka chairs around a campfire under the stars, or hiking through a forest clad in brilliant fall colors, or paddling a canoe under the moon while listening to the haunting call of the loon. These were all new experiences for us.

I would come to understand that there are some two million lakes scattered across Canada, more than anywhere else in the world. The greatest of the five Great Lakes, Lake Superior, contains enough water to flood all of North *and* South America to a depth of one foot. When you fly over the Northwest Territories and look down, it appears as if there are as many lakes below as there are stars in the sky.

In the United States, Bruce and I had very limited contact with Native Americans. But in Canada, we developed over time a huge network of Indigenous acquaintances and friends, including the national chief of the Assembly of First Nations, Perry Bellegarde, and his wife, Valerie Bellegarde. These friends and teachers showed us the warmth, patience, and kindness of the Indigenous people. They opened our eyes and afforded us first-hand experiences of the problems on reserves, such as ramshackle housing, crowded and underequipped schools, substandard health care, high unemployment, and soaring suicide rates. They told us about the Truth and Reconciliation Commission and how it worked with Indigenous communities to document the deplorable history of abuse and cultural genocide that resulted from the Indian Residential Schools Act, enacted in 1876. We learned that around 150,000 children and youth were taken from their families and homes and placed in residential schools during this dark period, which lasted well into the 1990s. School-related deaths were estimated in the thousands. I had to wonder, if Canada was able to recognize its past abuses of Indigenous people, why couldn't the United States do the same?

One First Nations man in Winnipeg spoke to us about the lasting legacy of the residential school system. "The trauma of that time is passed on from one generation to the next," he said. His anger grew as he shared his personal story. Finally, he demanded change and action and more spaces and places for the history of his people to be shared.

"I hear you," Bruce responded. "I hear what you're saying. I hear your need for space and land. I hear your need to tell your story and to reclaim your history. And I can tell you with all sincerity that your words have made a lasting impact."

Neither Bruce nor I will soon forget that visit. We could sense the desperation. These people wanted us to reach out to the Harper government. They wanted us to help them advocate for change. But we weren't in a position to give them what they wanted.

When I was in Kitchenuhmaykoosib Inninuwug First Nation (known as KI), a community of 1,200, I stayed in the home of Chief Donny Morris, one of six community leaders who had previously spent time in jail for protesting mining on traditional lands. I was moved by the chief and his community, by their will to survive, by their willingness to share their stories, and by their commitment to sustaining their community's traditional ways of life.

In Labrador, Bruce and I met with Natan Obed, the extraordinary young leader of the Inuit Tapiriit Kanatami (ITK), a non-profit organization that represents some sixty thousand Inuit in Canada. As a gifted hockey player and student, he attended Dartmouth College in New Hampshire on a scholarship. After returning to Canada, he became the leader of the ITK and created a suicide prevention program to address the horrific number of suicides among the Inuit youth.

While the pain and suffering of intergenerational trauma were so palpable and fresh, what was equally alive was the deep connection so many of the Indigenous people we met had with the land and the water. This connection is critical to everyone's survival. Many urban dwellers have lost it, but in remote places, that bond lives on, and so does the wisdom it offers. Nature can be our guide. Whether it's a small garden, a bee on a flower, an enormous, awe-inspiring lake—nature endures and sustains. Nature links individuals to their inner selves and helps them survive challenges, contemplate big questions, and find solutions. For me, the city does not eradicate my bond to nature—it just distracts me from it. I often visualize walking through groves of aspen trees on a beautiful, bright, windy day, and feeling while in that cathedral of trees that there is no more perfect, no more beautiful cathedral in the world. Nature is eternal. It's our connection to the past, present, and future. Nature is one reason why my connection to Canada—where nature is so accessible and where there are so many places of respite—is so deep.

There was a moment, before leaving the North, when Bruce and I, as a rite of passage, dipped our hands in the Arctic waters.

"This has been incredible and unforgettable," I said.

"It really has," he replied.

I dipped my hands in the Arctic waters before I left the North. It was a rite of passage and a reminder that in Canada, nature is accessible and can link us to our inner selves.

Chapter 6

Breaking the Ice

Bruce

As Vicki has shown, no matter where we went in that first year, we were greeted by people who opened their homes to us and invited us in; people who shared their love of their land, their businesses, and their communities. These were honest everyday Canadians. These were good citizens in cities and small towns who, upon getting to know us, were often forthright. They expressed to us their fears about climate change, sustainable agriculture, border issues, and trade. They told us their concerns about the United States and wanted more than anything to know that Americans shared their values. "We're neighbors," they said. "We're in this together. We need to build bridges, not walls."

Yes, dear Canada. That is what we needed to do in 2014. And that is what we need to do today, more than ever.

Our first year in Canada was full of learning and lessons. And while Vicki and I were becoming fast family with so many Canadians in Ottawa and across the country, our bridge building with the Harper government continued to be a challenge.

Upon arriving in Canada, it is customary for the U.S. ambassador and the prime minister to have a personal meeting, often a get-to-know-you dinner outside of regular government meetings.

"If we break bread, I know we'll be able to find common ground," Vicki said.

"Absolutely," I replied. "We've got to break bread—and we've got to break the ice."

"Bruce?"

"Yes, Vicki?"

"Break all the ice you want, but maybe don't mention again that you can't skate on it," she said with a smile.

Right. A good reminder.

As soon as we arrived in Ottawa, we sent a formal dinner invitation to the Harpers through the Protocol Office at the embassy. We waited awhile. "Unable to attend" was the response from the Prime Minister's Office. Spring turned to summer.

"Try again?" Vicki asked.

"For sure," I said.

Out went more invitations, some for intimate dinners, some for events at Lornado or the embassy. The response? Unable to attend.

"They must be *very* busy," Vicki said. "One more try?"

"Yes, one more." And off another invitation would go to the Prime Minister's Office.

Of course, we had a pretty good idea of what was going on. We were well aware that a message was being sent to Washington about our country's position on Keystone XL. We were the couriers. We were also well aware that we were Democrats, and the Harpers were Conservatives. Historically, the Canadian and American governments are most aligned when there's a Democratic ambassador and a Liberal Party government in power or a Republican ambassador and a Conservative Party

government. But while we were Obama's picks, we didn't feel our political differences should act as a roadblock. We were there to perform
our duties regardless of our political perspective or those of the government in power. Canada is a center-left country, and the United States
is a center-right country, but what's most important about that isn't the
difference but the similarity: we're both center.

We were told by the embassy that protocol was to dine with the
prime minister before extending invitations to the other party leaders.
But after the invitations to the Harpers were sent and declined, Vicki and
I decided to reach out to Justin Trudeau, then–Liberal leader of the opposition, and to his wife, Sophie Grégoire Trudeau. By this point, Vicki
and Sophie had met socially several times and had become friendly.
They would go for walks together. Sophie introduced Vicki to all the
paths and trails in Rockcliffe. Their immediate connection was born out
of love for family and for nature.

Getting together with the Trudeaus seemed like a natural thing one
does with people who have a lot in common. Whenever I ran into Justin
at the House of Commons, he'd throw open his arms in greeting. "Bruce,
it's so good to see you!" he'd say. He was the only party leader literally
coming to me with open arms.

"I hear Vicki and Sophie had a great walk last week," he once remarked.

"Yes, apparently there's some fox in the neighborhood that they've
both seen separately, and they're trying to track it down."

"More likely they're looking for excuses to have a nice stroll with
good company," Justin said.

"That sounds about right," I replied.

We waited and waited for either an acceptance of our dinner invitations to the Harpers or an invitation from them. Eventually it was just
too much waiting. I simply informed the U.S. embassy that we had a
date for dinner with the Trudeaus in the fall of 2014. If a dinner with the
Harpers were to happen, it was yet to be determined.

Justin Trudeau greeted me with open arms whenever I would meet him in the House of Commons.

The Art of Diplomacy

We dined with the Trudeaus in Lornado, but not in the formal dining room. The living room of the residence had stunning bay windows that looked out over the river and the Gatineau Hills. We had a small table there that seated four, which was perfect for this intimate and casual dinner.

What I remember most about that night is Justin recounting the story of how he and Conservative Senator Patrick Brazeau had boxed each other for charity in 2012. Their participation in the fifth annual Fight for the Cure raised more than $200,000 for the Ottawa Regional Cancer Foundation. Although this was a charity event, Justin told me, it was also a serious fight. In the lead-up to the match, Brazeau began trash-talking, claiming that he doubted his Liberal opponent could take a punch, and, in fact, most people favored Brazeau to win. After all, the senator had a black belt in karate and had once served in the Canadian Naval Reserve.

So what did Trudeau do? He trained. He practiced. He prepared. And as he told me the story, he made sure that I understood what he was really saying: that he was not afraid of hard work; that even though he was the underdog, he should not be underestimated; and that, make no mistake, he was a competitor.

"Sophie, I've got this," is what he said before the bout.

"Did you have reservations?" Vicki asked Sophie.

"Of course I did!" she answered.

After three rounds, with Brazeau's nose bleeding from the pummeling of Trudeau's gloves, the referee called the match. There was a clear victor. Trudeau had won.

Beyond boxing, Justin and I talked about many things that night. What was clear to me even then was that he was a man of conviction; someone who was authentic, honest, and had a clear perspective of what he wanted for Canada—and what he didn't. He did not come out and say he would win in the next election, but he made it abundantly clear that no matter what happened, he would never be a pushover. The press didn't always take him seriously, poking fun at his perfect hair and his good looks and his fondness for yoga, but the impression both Vicki and I were left with after that night was that this was a man with integrity and tenacity. This was a contender.

"When was the last time you met someone with that kind of leadership potential?" I asked Vicki after the Trudeaus had left.

"In 2006. His name was Barack Obama," she replied.

"But do you think he can do it? Can he actually win in the next election?" I knew exactly what she would say.

"Yes. He. Can."

That fall, I had many encounters with Stephen Harper and his associates, though not of the social kind. In September 2014, while I was in Ottawa, the prime minister was in New York at Goldman Sachs being interviewed by *The Wall Street Journal* in the very same conference room where I had once attended so many meetings. Life can be strange like that. It was the night before the Jewish New Year, so when the embassy rang my cell phone as I sat in the library at Lornado, I was a little surprised.

"Mr. Ambassador, I'm sorry to disturb you. Are you aware of what Harper said to the press today?"

"Well, I've kind of been a little off-line this evening for the Jewish holiday," I answered.

"Sir, I need you to know that Harper announced today that the U.S. government asked Canada to join the bombing campaign in Iraq."

"I'm sorry?" I said. I couldn't believe what I was hearing. "I'm not aware of any such request. Don't you think we would have been briefed if that were the case?"

"Well, that's why we're calling. You're sure you or someone from the embassy hasn't had any side conversation with the Prime Minister's Office on this subject?"

I was certain, of course, that we had not. No one at the PMO was

Bruce and I graduating from Vanderbilt University. From the beginning, we worked together to reach the same goal.

With thumbs up to the new sign, we say good-bye to Chicago before heading off to Canada.

The future President and First Lady at a campaign fund-raiser at our Lincoln Park home. Our friend took this photo of the Obamas; and when she sent the photo to Michelle, she received a beautiful handwritten note thanking her for capturing this moment.

With our daughter Caroline at President Obama's birthday fund-raiser at his home in Hyde Park, Chicago.

Election Night 2012. Celebrating President Obama's re-election and his vision of a unified America.

When Vice President Joe Biden officiated Bruce's swearing-in, beaming from ear to ear, he said, "Lucky Canada and lucky U.S. We are getting a twofer." Here we are surrounded by family (*from left to right*): David Heyman, our son; me; Alison Ayer Heyman, our daughter-in-law; Sherry Heyman, Bruce's mom; Liza Heyman MacCarthy, our oldest daughter; Caroline Heyman Rudzki, our youngest daughter; and Vice President Joe Biden.

At Rideau Hall, with the Governor General's Foot Guards in their bearskin hats on the day Bruce officially became U.S. ambassador to Canada.

Meeting Prime Minister Stephen Harper for the first time in his office. He was prime minister for the first eighteen months of our tenure.

Entering the National Gallery of Canada the evening Bruce gave his first official address.

Greeting the new prime minister of Canada, Justin Trudeau, and his wife, Sophie, in Parliament at their first holiday party in December 2015.

Welcoming a Mountie at our Kentucky Derby party at Lornado. Notice the bare trees and bushes—spring hadn't quite reached Ottawa yet.

In the library of our official residence, Lornado, Bruce and I surrounded ourselves with art that evoked conversation among the many guests who visited. A Chuck Close portrait of Obama graces the wall behind me, civil rights photographs by Ernest Withers are on the right wall, and Bruce is leaning on Marie Watt's inspiring blanket sculpture.

A healthy hive: the exchange of ideas binds communities. We hosted salons at Lornado to encourage dialogue between Americans and Canadians.

Laughing and chatting: it was clear from the beginning that Bruce and Prime Minister Justin Trudeau were going to be able to work together on behalf of both of our nations.

After arriving in the United States, Bruce's grandfather Sam was drafted into World War I. Bruce displayed his grandfather's U.S. Army uniform in his embassy office as tribute to his service.

Sharing Le Jardin de Lornado with young guests. In the garden, we planted over sixty different varieties of fruits and vegetables. My favorite was the giant pumpkins.

Do as the Canadians do: Bruce enthusiastically trying a Canadian treat in the ByWard Market in Ottawa.

Happy Heymans! Celebrating America's birthday from the stage with our daughters, Caroline and Liza.

Madame Donna Chevrier of Ola Cocina, one of our favorite Ottawa restaurants, with me and Heyman Hot Sauce in hand.

Tumbling Woman in the embassy's atrium: we brought Eric Fischl's controversial sculpture to the U.S. embassy. It elicited strong reactions and led to many healing conversations.

Standing in front of a powerful watercolor of *Tumbling Woman* by Eric Fischl at Lornado.

Grooving with Madame Michaëlle Jean celebrating a successful Power of the Arts National Forum in 2015.

Bruce and I learned the art of beekeeping at Ted Norris's bee farm in Kemptville, Ontario. We brought hives to Lornado as a way to participate in the National Pollinator Strategy, an action plan to increase bee-friendly habitats.

Remembrance Day in Ottawa, paying respect to those who sacrificed so much.

Bruce with President Obama in the Oval Office. In President Obama's speech to Parliament in 2017, he said, "The world needs more Canada." His words underlined the importance of the Canada-U.S. partnership.

The three-day state visit by Prime Minister Justin Trudeau to Washington was a huge success. Before the state dinner, we joined the Trudeau and Obama families at the White House on the Truman balcony. Here, Sophie Grégoire Trudeau and I enjoy the moment.

The diplomacy of art: during our time in Canada, Bruce and I worked together to open doors, protect shared resources, and celebrate art. Installation by Carlos Amorales at The Power Plant in Toronto.

Our last July Fourth at Lornado, dancing the night away with our granddaughters, Clara and Emma.

A moment of levity during President Obama's visit to Parliament.

Friends supporting friends after the Pulse nightclub shooting in Orlando, Florida.

Before departing Ottawa, I worked with the U.S. embassy to commission this iconic photograph of Parliament Hill on Canada Day by American artist Stephen Wilkes—a gift to Canada to celebrate their 150th anniversary of Confederation.

answering our requests for meetings. It was entirely possible that someone in Washington had spoken with someone in the Canadian government regarding this issue, but the embassy and I knew nothing about it.

The call ended after that, and I remained stunned. Soon after, the
Canadian media began pressuring the Harper government, asking the
obvious question: "Who from the White House made this request for
Canada to join in Iraq?"

The Canadian media and the Harper government spent the next
twenty-four hours going back and forth about who'd asked whom
to help with the Iraq war, by then in its eleventh year. The embassy
watched the Ping-Pong match while declining the many media requests
for clarity.

It was obvious to me that Prime Minister Harper and his team were
in a bit of a jam.

While walking to the embassy the next morning, I had an idea that
could help the situation. I was slated to be on *The Evan Solomon Show*
that weekend, so I called Harper's chief of staff, Raymond Novak.

"Ray," I said, "I've been following what's happened in the last twenty-
four hours, and we don't want to create more problems here, when we're
both on the same side. I'm thinking maybe I can offer some assistance.
Perhaps it would be helpful if I were to issue some kind of statement on
Evan's radio show this weekend that clarifies the United States would be
open to receiving help in Iraq?"

Pause. Perhaps he was thinking this through and coming to the
conclusion that it would be a good solution.

"Let me talk to the comms team," he said finally. "We'll get back
to you."

And this time the Prime Minister's Office did get back to us. After
some conversation with my staff and with Washington, I decided that
I wouldn't wait for the weekend to release a statement. I'd do so right
away. I started with a Canadian Press news agency interview by phone.
Then I did a sweep of television with the same message:

"On behalf of the U.S. government, I'd like to invite Canada to participate in the Iraq effort," I said.

"And can you tell us, Mr. Ambassador, what it is specifically that the United States is looking for in terms of support?"

"I think we'll leave that up to the Canadian government. We'll let them decide how they'd like to participate, but let me be clear: any and all help from Canada in the U.S.-led campaign against ISIS would be deeply appreciated by the United States."

"Mr. Ambassador, can I ask for some clarification? Did your government ask Canada to join the efforts in Iraq, or did Canada first ask you if they could participate?"

"It's not really consequential who asked whom first," I replied. "Our government representatives have discussions all the time. The fact that Canada wants to help—that's what's important."

And so it went. I did a version of this interview, with roughly the same answers, approximately ten times. I became the bridge on the issue of support for military strikes in Iraq. And within twenty-four hours, the entire issue of who asked whom fizzled out and disappeared. Shortly thereafter, Stephen Harper stood in the House of Commons and promised to work closely with Americans and other allies in airstrikes in Iraq.

After that, everything opened up for me in Ottawa. When I asked for meetings with cabinet ministers, I got them. I was able to work with the various ministries and forge relationships. Meanwhile, Vicki was blazing her own trail, and the doors were opening for her, too. She'd met with Laureen Harper at a couple of social events, and in November 2014 she had tea with her in our home. She learned that Laureen was a very outgoing and expressive person. She was open with Vicki about her upbringing and conveyed great pride in her family. The eldest of three, Laureen was born in Turner Valley, a rural town southwest of Calgary. She grew up on a family ranch, which instilled in her an appreciation of nature and a love of animals.

Vicki was impressed by Laureen's strength and candor. It was clear that she was her own person—an engaged woman with goals and aspirations, a woman who'd made a lot of sacrifices, too.

That tea lasted well over a couple of hours, and as Vicki says, "It was another source of warmth, another bridge built."

The ice was beginning to melt.

Here is a truth that ambassadors and diplomats—and husbands and wives—know all too well: you can change a relationship, but to do so takes time. Diplomacy can and does work, but it takes patient communication. It takes careful listening and a clear-eyed assessment of both what's being asked and what it is you are able to offer.

When I think of the great ambassadors who have risen to the highest standards of the office, I think of Ken Taylor. Ken was the Canadian ambassador to Iran best known for his role in the Iranian hostage crisis. On November 4, 1979, Iranian students stormed the U.S. embassy in Tehran, taking more than fifty hostages. Six Americans were able to escape that day and, over the course of four days, painstakingly make their way to the Canadian embassy. There they were offered refuge by Ambassador Taylor and his embassy team. The only problem was how to get those escapees out of the embassy and back to the safety of America. Ken personally housed some of them in his home over several weeks. He became involved in the operation now known as the "Canadian Caper," an elaborate scheme to procure six Canadian passports for the Americans and to have them pose as a Canadian film crew scouting locations for a shoot, thereby deceiving the Iranian Revolutionary Guard—the arm of the military loyal to the country's new religious leader, Ayatollah Ruhollah Khomeini. The covert operation succeeded, and the six Americans were able to board a plane and return home in early 1980.

I first met Ken in New York in April 2014, when I was there to present an award to Canadian-born American architect Frank Gehry on behalf of the Council for Canadian American Relations. I was so excited to meet him. This man was a hero, and I felt I was in the presence of someone incredibly special.

"Ken, I hope you'll come to Ottawa," I said. "I'd love for you to come to our party at Lornado on the Fourth of July."

Always soft-spoken, always kind, Ken said, "I'd love to. That would be great."

Wow. I couldn't believe it. When I returned to Ottawa, I sent off an invitation, but in the back of my mind, I was thinking, *Maybe he was just being polite. He probably won't come.*

Lo and behold, he came. We enjoyed a spectacular Fourth of July party, which we called the Great American Picnic and which drew some three thousand guests, many of them dressed in summer whites. We had invited the Harpers and all of his cabinet ministers, but very few showed up. However, we were honored to have former prime minister Joe Clark and his wife, Maureen McTeer, among our guests, proof that we were happy to extend an olive branch to politicians of all affiliations, and proof, too, that some extended the branch back. And Ken Taylor was also there with us that day. We had a chance to have several private conversations, all of which were unforgettable.

I asked him about the films that had been made about the events in Tehran, both the 1981 TV movie *Escape from Iran: The Canadian Caper* and *Argo*, which won the Academy Award for best picture of 2012. "Were they accurate?" I wanted to know.

In his humble, unassuming way, Ken shrugged his shoulders and said, "Movies are movies, Bruce. Yes, some things are accurate; others aren't."

"Ken," I said, "what you did . . . you're a hero. You took such a huge risk, and not even for citizens of your own country. You not only stepped in, you stepped up. You were there when we needed you. You helped six Americans escape with their lives."

Ken would have none of it. "I just did what anyone would do. You would have done the same if you were in my place. It didn't matter to

Ken Taylor, Canadian ambassador to Iran, who heroically rescued six Americans during the Iranian Hostage Crisis in 1979. He was a true hero and a great friend.

me that they weren't Canadians. They were people. We're all just people, Bruce, when it comes down to it."

How true and wise. I hoped Ken was right. I hoped that if I ever faced a situation anything like the one Ken had found himself in, I, too, would step up.

For the entire time he was in our presence, Vicki and I could not help ourselves. "Do you know who that is over there?" we'd say to one guest after another. "That's Ken Taylor!"

"*The* Ken Taylor?" they'd reply. And we'd nod vigorously. Our guests, many from the United States, would instantly make a beeline to shake his hand.

In October 2015 Ken died of cancer. I was asked to speak at the memorial service following his funeral, which took place in Toronto. Some of those six Americans he'd helped rescue were there to pay their respects. I paid tribute to him as a hero to both Canadians and Americans. I talked about how he exemplified the best of the U.S.-Canada relationship. I expressed how much he'd meant to me personally, and how much all of us—his friends, his family, and the many people around the world who'd been touched by him—would miss him. I presented his wife, Pat, with an American flag that we had flown at the U.S. embassy in Ottawa.

"Ken was a Canadian hero and friend to Americans and to all people," I said to her. "And he will be remembered fondly always."

It is normal, I think, for those with great responsibilities placed on their shoulders to wonder what they would do in a crisis. In Ken's case, he was a mild-mannered man who, upon first glance, did not appear to be a maverick risk taker. And yet when called upon, he stepped up. When I think about Ken, sometimes I think, too, about President Obama and the weight that was on his shoulders throughout his two terms of office. It's hard to imagine that level of responsibility and what kind of pressure it places on a leader.

I vividly recall a time when I got a first-hand understanding of

Obama's foremost concerns. Once, in my presence, the president was asked what most robbed him of sleep. At that moment, it wasn't terrorism or a natural disaster. It was the fear of a global pandemic. Ebola virus, swine flu, Zika virus, SARS—these were very high on his list of anxieties. Obama worried about our country's—and the world's—lack of preparedness if faced with such threats. Once here, a pandemic would be difficult to contain. It takes planning in advance to keep a pandemic at bay. Also, as with a forest fire, it's much easier to put out a small flame and so much harder to extinguish an inferno.

The Ebola outbreak in West Africa between 2014 and 2016 killed eleven thousand people and infected twenty-eight thousand more, making it the largest and the most complex epidemic since the virus was discovered in 1976.

The United States and its rapid response team took the lead in controlling the spread of the virus. Virtually every American ambassador in the world, including me, was asked by the State Department about approaching his or her host country for assistance in containing the spread. The U.S. military built landing strips where needed in Africa to ship in supplies. They quarantined infected communities. They buried the dead. They provided aid to the living. Americans at home raised money and awareness.

The United States and Canada work together in many obvious and highly visible ways. Think of NATO and NORAD and our common border—all examples of co-operation. But there are many ways our two countries co-operate behind the scenes, addressing problems or engaging in opportunities. With the Ebola outbreak, our synergies were at play again.

In the beginning of my tenure, the Ebola crisis was more or less off the radar, but as it spread, I appealed directly to Canada's minister of health, Rona Ambrose, for help. I knew that Prime Minister Harper was focused on maternal health as a global issue, and Ebola was striking women and babies in West Africa. That made it easier to pitch a compelling argument for why Canada should participate in containment and aid efforts. I made a number of suggestions on how it could be helpful to the cause.

Rona Ambrose stepped up to the plate, with an initial offering of $35 million on Canada's behalf, and then, on October 17, 2014, another $30 million to support international efforts led by the United Nations Mission for Ebola Emergency Response (UNMEER). I was very pleased with our collaboration on this effort—proof yet again of what two countries can accomplish by working together. You can't wait until a pandemic is out of control.

I'm very troubled about the role of the United States in the world today and the way we are failing to coalesce when global threats arise. If there is another outbreak of Ebola or another virus, I'm not satisfied we'll be quick enough to put resources where they're needed to reduce the risk. To tackle an impending epidemic or similar global threat requires strong partnerships with global allies. President Trump has treated Canada and other key allies in transactional terms. This hinders relationships and makes rapid response difficult, which is why I'm concerned should an unanticipated global crisis arise during Trump's term of office.

I also see a diminished role for ambassadors now. A full year into the Trump presidency, close to 25 percent of ambassadorships were not filled. In January 2018 *The Washington Post* reported that some 245 important diplomatic posts remained vacant. In fact, the State Department claims the most unfilled political jobs in the cabinet. Another equally concerning issue is the post-Trump departure of so many talented career diplomats from around the world. Ambassadors, deputy chiefs of mission, and others who submitted resignations will not easily be replaced. This has left the United States with diminished talent and experience in the complex work of diplomacy.

What does all of this mean? The current U.S. administration shows little interest in taking a global lead. And while Obama lost sleep about

Ebola during his time in office, I think many Americans, myself included, now worry about what we would do in the event of a major viral outbreak or other global threat. More than ever, we need allies. We need to sit down at the same table and work through issues together. More than ever, we need to stay vigilant and united.

In March 2015, about a year into my term of office, the Canadian newspaper *The Globe and Mail* published an article with the headline "How Ottawa Left U.S. Ambassador Bruce Heyman Out in the Cold." In it, journalist Campbell Clark referred to how I'd had a "rough" first year as ambassador. He cited differences in opinion with the Harper government over the Keystone XL pipeline and who would pay for the U.S. customs plaza for the proposed bridge between Windsor and Detroit. And he was right: both of those issues presented challenges. He also pointed to the fact that my chilly reception from the Canadian government was not typical for new American ambassadors to Canada, writing: "In the 1990s, Gordon Giffin sipped Scotch with Jean Chrétien. Mr. Obama's first envoy, David Jacobson, went snowshoeing with Laureen Harper. Canadian governments usually worked on the relationship." Again, all true.

But what wasn't entirely accurate was that the freeze had lasted for a full year. In fact, by the time the article was published, doors were opening, productive meetings were happening, and diplomatic relations were starting to normalize—though that was not entirely obvious to the public at large. Also, many U.S. governors came north for trade missions after receiving my letter highlighting the trade his or her state engaged in with Canada. As I said to the Canadian Press at the time, "I'm having the meetings that are necessary for me to have. I feel very comfortable that we're driving outcomes in our bilateral relationship."

But the press kept pointing out one thing: that I'd met directly with the prime minister only twice. Fair point.

Perhaps all of this media coverage contributed to the end of the ice age and, finally, to the full warming of the waters. In July 2015 Vicki and I received an invitation from the Prime Minister's Office for a private dinner with Stephen and Laureen at the official residence that has no nickname and is known as 24 Sussex Drive. We were delighted to accept.

The night we went there, Stephen was getting over a cold and was still feeling a little under the weather, but it was clear he wanted to have this dinner.

As a gift, we brought a book about American architect Frank Lloyd Wright.

"What a lovely gesture," Laureen said. "Thank you so much."

We enjoyed a pleasant evening. Fortunately, by this time, Laureen and Vicki knew each other a bit, and both being women with a gift for conversation, they were able to bridge the divide in a natural and sincere way.

Vicki was talking about her amazing trip to Kitchenuhmaykoosib Inninuwug First Nation, a three-hour plane ride north of Thunder Bay, Ontario.

"You went *where*?" Stephen said. He seemed surprised and impressed that Vicki's explorations were as far ranging as they were.

"The people I met were so warm, and they shared their culture with me so generously," Vicki said. "Though I have to say that it's disturbing to see the problems on the reserves: the ramshackle housing, under-equipped schools, and substandard health care."

"Where did you stay?" Laureen asked.

"With Chief Donny Morris," I replied.

Silence. Chief Donny Morris was a strong and gracious man who stood up for the rights and beliefs of his people.

Stephen pursued a new line of questioning. "And how would you characterize Canada so far?" he asked. "If you were to describe it in a word, what would it be?"

Vicki paused and thought about it. "Exotic," she said.

Stephen and Laureen looked at each other. Maybe they were puzzled.

"Yes, exotic from coast to coast to coast," Vicki said. "Your country is full of treasures—natural, traditional, humanistic, artistic—and I never knew that before, at least not the depth and breadth. I've encountered many great Canadian teachers and guides all across the country. It's been a wonderful voyage of discovery.

"And what about you, Prime Minister? You've had this extraordinary opportunity to lead your country, to go everywhere, to do anything. When you close your eyes and you think about a cherished memory on your foreign journeys, what is it?"

He turned to her with a smile on his face and said, "I remember when I went to Abbey Road in the UK, and I sat at the piano there and played." That the prime minister loved the Beatles was clear from the expression on his face as he revisited this memory of the recording studio where the group had created so many classic songs.

"That's amazing!" I said. "What a moment."

He nodded and smiled again. "It was pretty great." And in that instant, we felt the real Stephen Harper emerge—a bit of the person behind the politician.

I decided to tell the Harpers my story of going to Ola Cocina in Ottawa and how the owner, Madame Chevrier, had not believed I was the ambassador.

They laughed, and this led to a discussion of hot sauces.

"Hold on just a moment," Laureen said. "Let me call out our chef." Out he came. "Our guests here love hot sauces, so can we sample a few?"

"Of course," he said. "I'll put a selection together."

Out came an array of hot sauces created, prepared, and served at 24 Sussex, with more spice and flavor than you could ever imagine.

"Try this one," the prime minister said, and we did.

It tasted mild at first, but after a while, it got surprisingly hot and fiery.

All in all, it was a lovely evening, and it was clear that the four of us were doing our best to build a new bridge. And with the help of the hot sauces of 24 Sussex, the ice age in relations had finally thawed.

Chapter 7

A Healthy Hive

Vicki

Have you ever looked at a honeycomb up close? It is one of the most aesthetically pleasing and wondrous sights in the natural world. The comb is where bees save and store honey and pollen, and where they create a nursery for the next generation of bees. The hexagonal cells that make up the comb are orderly and symmetrical. They are strong and support one another. No comb exists on its own. Each shares a wall with another comb. Put all of the sides together, and you have a geometric shape with myriad functions, but its chief purpose is to serve as the hub of community life.

To connect people, you need a connecting mechanism. That's the hive-and-honeycomb model applied to humans. Bees know it well. It's in their nature to create community; to work toward the betterment of the hive and all the bees that live in it. This is a model that speaks to me. The hive model worked during my days fund-raising in Chicago, and it worked for the entire team that helped get Barack Obama elected president. There is no energy more powerful than collective energy. And rather than building something on your own, you can be much more effective when you enlist the aid of people who believe in your idea and are capable of building their own honeycombs. Cell by cell, the reach becomes exponential.

One of the first things I did in Ottawa was to write down on my office whiteboard the names of the influencers, the movers and shakers, the change makers and agitators in the arts, in communities, and in political circles. I did the same for Montreal, Vancouver, and Toronto. And the more I traveled the country, the more people I added to my list—not only those from urban centers but also those from all places big and small. Canada is filled with people of influence, be they famous or little known. They leave their indelible mark on the social, cultural, and political fabric of the country. They create hives. It didn't take long for my whiteboard to become too crowded. Eventually, as I met more leaders and influencers, and as I included the many institutions I got to know, I moved from cataloguing on the board to keeping a database that served as my record of who was who and how they were making a positive impact.

Remember that old acronym NIMBY—not in my backyard? NIMBYs are those who don't want anything to disturb the sanctity of their borders. It is so easy for us to become NIMBYs. But as Bruce and I traveled across Canada, we discovered people who promoted the hive mentality rather than the NIMBY one. These were people who chose to give back, to engage with their communities, to stand up and say: here in our backyard is a problem we would like to solve. Such people speak up in the face of injustice. They ask questions. They empathize. They nurture democracy, and they find their own voice to impact the world. We met change makers seeking innovative solutions to social problems, who wanted to enrich society through disseminating bold ideas. Today ideas can flow freely. No walls could ever impede that flow. I felt called to be part of that open exchange of ideas. My contribution was to arts and culture. I wanted Canadian change makers to inspire and form connections with leaders and movements in the United States. Why? Because positive change knows no border and needs no passport.

In 2015 I created a series called Contemporary Conversations with the help of my chief of staff, Gillian Catrambone. Gillian worked side by side with me in our home office in Lornado. She was my collaborator and partner in all things Canada. We learned, laughed, and dreamed together. In the first year of Contemporary Conversations, we featured four pre-eminent American artists and their works, presented by the U.S. embassy and Art in Embassies in partnership with the amazing team directed by Marc Mayer at the National Gallery in Ottawa. The Art in Embassies program had brought American art around the world for years, but with this new program, I wanted to bring the artists themselves along with their works to Canada so that true conversations and connections could happen. I sought artists whose work examined borderless issues: social justice, equality, the environment, and identity. That first year, we brought Marie Watt, Nick Cave, Eric Fischl, and Stephen Wilkes to Ottawa to talk about their work, which was on display at our residence and in the National Gallery.

I have never been the kind of person who thinks of art as something simply to hang on the wall. Art is not décor. It is not just a pleasing backdrop. It is not meant to blend in. True art and true artists are subversive and explosive. Artists are truth tellers who hold up a mirror to the problems in our society. Their voices and their work are critically important, now more than ever, when confidence and belief in our political and corporate leadership are suspect. Art ignites conversation. It inspires change. It allows a secret passage to open where no access point appeared before. It's hard to have engaging and meaningful discussion around controversial topics, but through the lens of art, we can approach sensitive issues with openness, willingness, and awareness.

I could, for example, try to convince you of the truth about climate change, or I could show you a photograph by Canadian artist Edward Burtynsky, such as *Colorado River Delta #2*, which hung at Lornado during our tenure. Renowned for his aerial images, Burtynsky has spent the greater part of three decades capturing what he describes as "nature, transformed through industry," or manufactured industrial landscapes. His work urges us to think about the human impact on the environment and about climate change. It serves as a powerful reminder that our natural resources are finite and need protection. In his words, "We have to learn to think more long term about the consequences of what we are doing while we are doing it. My hope is that these pictures will stimulate a process of thinking about something essential to our survival; something we often take for granted—until it's gone."[1]

Art, at its best, is storytelling that conveys truth. My tactic has long been to use storytelling as the glue to create community. Story: that's what people remember.

The first artist we brought to Ottawa as part of Contemporary Conversations was multidisciplinary artist Marie Watt from Portland, Oregon. Marie's bloodlines are Indigenous (the Turtle Clan of the Seneca Nation) and immigrant settler (Scottish, German, Wyoming rancher). She defines herself as "half cowboy, half Indian." Her work involves textiles, and in particular, blankets.

As she has said, "I'm interested in how blankets are objects that we take for granted, but they can have extraordinary histories."[2]

Her work is often made of gifted and scavenged blankets, many of them handmade, discarded, or found in thrift stores. Using blankets piled on top of each other, she creates powerful, looming pillars with sculptural integrity and surreal strength. Each blanket is the story of a family or a generation, and stacked together, they have a resonant presence. Some have called them totems.

"Blankets are also personal to me," Marie said in an artist's statement

Marie Watt's blanket tower in our library in Lornado.

about her work. "My tribe gives blankets away to honor people for standing witness to important life events."[3]

One of Marie's pieces graced our library at Lornado: *Skywalker/Skyscraper*, an eight-foot-tall pile of neatly folded, intricately woven blankets with a gray steel beam rising up from it. The blankets were old and well used; they had stories to tell. Each was carefully folded and positioned in the formidable stack. Marie also had a sculpture in the National Gallery of Canada: a thirty-five-foot totem of gifted blankets, and each had a small card attached containing a few lines about its history. One was from a concentration camp; another was from a baby's crib; yet another was a discarded family heirloom rescued from the Salvation Army.

We kept Marie busy while she was in Canada. She delivered a lecture on her work, gave several interviews with journalists, and hosted a sewing circle. She also participated in a seminar at Ottawa's Carleton University with Indigenous artists and curators. They explored the challenges of caring for and presenting Indigenous work in gallery spaces. It was at this seminar that I first learned that Indigenous masks embody spirits and that they not only should be treated as art but also cared for as sacred objects. Marie has talked in interviews about her sewing circles and why she created them.

"When I host a sewing circle, I invite people of all ages to come, no sewing experience necessary. . . . I'm interested in how everyone's stitch is unique, kind of like a thumbprint or a signature. . . . When the stitches start to intersect, they're a metaphor for how we're all connected and related."[4]

The sewing circle took place at a hundred-foot-long table in the National Gallery rotunda. A free event, like all events in the Contemporary Conversation series, it attracted more than two hundred participants. Community members from all backgrounds—children, artists, students, young and old—all took up needle and thread on that cold, wintry Saturday morning in February. People worked elbow to elbow, offering proof of what Marie had often said: that stitching together on

The sewing circle at the National Gallery of Canada filled the room with hundreds of people coming together to celebrate art and share their stories.

something as ordinary as cloth allows personal exchanges to occur and stories to be told.

Bruce came out that day to join the sewing circle.

"Marie, I don't know what I'm doing," he admitted readily. "I'm a bit embarrassed to tell you this, but I have never sewn in my life."

"Not to worry," she replied. "Have a seat. It's time for you to learn something new."

I watched from across the table as Bruce threaded his first needle and learned the running stitch. Before long, he was engaged in animated conversation with the other sewers around him even as he labored over his line on the fabric.

And this is how it is done, I thought to myself. *One change, one story, one stitch at a time.*

"How do you drop the barrier to be open to something that is 'other'?"

It's a very big question, and it's one where art itself might be the answer.

But I was not the one to ask the question. It was asked by Nick Cave, the renowned American multidisciplinary artist. Nick's mystical creations, which he calls soundsuits, began in reaction to the brutal and senseless beating of Rodney King in 1991 by Los Angeles police. That assault—and the fact that the four officers involved were acquitted the following year despite undeniable video proof of their brutality— provoked a series of deadly riots in Los Angeles and outrage across the world. For Nick Cave, it flipped his world upside down. He recalls sitting traumatized in Chicago's Grant Park after the L.A. riots. He was thinking about media portrayals of Rodney King as a kind of monster. "They described him as larger than life, scary, and that it took ten policemen to bring him down. I started thinking, *What does that look like? And how do I identify myself as a black male?* I was thinking, *The moment I leave my studio, my identity is in jeopardy.*"[5]

At that point, he looked down and saw a twig on the ground. He picked it up, and it spawned an idea. What if, through found objects, through the detritus the world casts off or ignores, he could build himself a form of protection: a suit that would arm him against the threats of the outside world?

"It is like building a second skin that hides gender, race, class, and forces you to look without judgment," Cave explained in *The Huffington Post*.[6]

Once he created his first suit, made fully out of twigs, he put it on. It was then that he realized the suit made a sound—his armor had its very own voice. He has since gone on to make soundsuits out of a variety of found materials, including dyed human hair, sisal, plastic buttons, beads, sequins, and feathers—and to perform dance pieces while wearing his artistic creations.

I was lucky enough to meet Nick in Chicago almost a decade ago, and I knew he was exactly the right voice to bring to Canada. In May 2015 he came to speak at the National Gallery and to be involved with youth from the Youth Services Bureau of Ottawa and Le Lab in Gatineau, an artistic organization for at-risk young people. The night of the gallery event, the auditorium was packed. As I peeked between the curtains before Nick went onstage, I was thrilled to see so many young, fresh faces in the audience.

Nick is soft-spoken and an arrestingly good-looking man with a dancer's grace and strength. He spoke onstage with the museum's assistant curator, Jonathan Shaughnessy, about his life: he'd grown up poor, one of six brothers in Fulton, Missouri, raised by his single mother. He talked about his identity as well as his artistic journey through dance and later art. At one point, Jonathan said, "You yourself talk about being a messenger."

Nick paused. "That's what I am," he said. "There was a moment in my life when I was just running from my truth. So I think that when I stopped running, I just . . . changed." His voice caught and tears sprang to his eyes. "My whole life changed one night. I just came into an acceptance."[7]

Standing with multidisciplinary artist Nick Cave and visual artist Bob Faust at Lornado. We brought American artists whose work examined borderless issues. Behind us is one of Nick's incredible soundsuits.

Art institutions, unfortunately, can be scary spaces for some people, especially for youth. So when it was time for questions, I was concerned that people would hesitate. As it turned out, I had nothing to worry about. Nick had been authentic, open, and honest, and the audience saw in him an invitation to speak about their own experiences of social alienation and segregation. One brave young woman stood up and said she was wrestling with her identity.

"Was it hard for you to come out as a gay man?" she asked point-blank.

"Girlfriend," Nick said, "it was not hard coming out, but it *was* hard having all these identity issues as an African American man, as an artist living in a small community in the United States. *That* was hard."

He also talked about what it was like putting on a soundsuit. He described it as a transformative process. "You can be a hot mess, but if you are fearless, that's enormous. I see potential there."

Following Nick's talk, one of the young people in the audience wrote about her experience. She said she felt a sense of belonging simply by being in the crowd with an artist who was as "non-conventional" as she felt herself to be. It seemed that this event marked an advancement in her personal artistic path.

And that is the power of art and artists.

In 2002 artist Eric Fischl's controversial bronze sculpture *Tumbling Woman* became the object of much outrage and controversy. The life-sized piece depicts a nude woman who appears to be in midfall, her vulnerability caught moments before she hits the ground. *Tumbling Woman* was intended to commemorate the victims of 9/11 and was slated to be displayed at Rockefeller Center in New York City for several months, but within days of being installed, many expressed their anger about this piece.

Some said it was tasteless and insensitive. Others accused the artist of profiting from their loss.

As for Eric, he was shocked and saddened by how his work had been received. "The sculpture was not meant to hurt anybody," he stated. "It was an expression of deepest sympathy for the vulnerability of the human condition, both toward the victims of 9/11 and toward humanity in general."[8]

The case for its removal was taken up by New York's tabloid newspapers, and just days after the statue was installed, it was curtained off and then unceremoniously removed.

For the artist, this was devastating on many fronts.

By the time we brought Eric to Ottawa for Contemporary Conversations, thirteen years had passed since *Tumbling Woman* was first displayed in Rockefeller Center. We had Eric come to speak in early September so that we could open up a conversation about 9/11 and also recognize the incredible role that Canadians played supporting America after the attacks. We had three days with Eric, and that gave us a chance to know him as the deep thinker he is. He is a witty man, smart and provocative, kind and talkative, very comfortable in his own shoes. That being said, there was still some trepidation about *Tumbling Woman* and how it would be received. Would Canadians see the intention behind the work? Had enough time passed for a healing discussion to occur?

There were some raised eyebrows when I made the initial proposal to the embassy. "Are you sure you want to use Contemporary Conversations to address 9/11?" I was asked. "And are you sure this particular artist will be well received?"

While some people in the embassy community were concerned, I was confident that Eric would be well received, and I was certain that opening up the conversation was the right thing to do. When I accompanied him into the National Gallery to see the installation of *Tumbling Woman* (a beautiful version that Eric had made in Plexiglas), I was full of anticipation and excitement—and I suspect Eric was as well. Our steps echoed as we made our way down the long, cavernous corridor. Then

Eric Fischl's *Tumbling Woman* in Plexiglas at the National Gallery of Canada. The placement of the sculpture brought tears to Eric's eyes.

we entered the rotunda, where the piece was displayed. Set between two tall, majestic pillars, the sculpture was bathed in warm sunlight from above. It looked ethereal; almost angelic. I had a small glass maquette of *Tumbling Woman* in Lornado, but to see the life-sized version took my breath away.

I saw tears come to Eric's eyes. "The columns. They remind me of the Twin Towers."

"Oh my," I said. "You're right."

We stood silently, taking in *Tumbling Woman* and feeling both the gravity of the moment and of her fall.

Later, when Bruce interviewed Eric for a commemorative video, he asked him to talk about why he'd created the piece.

Eric said he'd wanted to "participate in the mourning process the country was going through. . . . [It] felt like the country had gone off balance and become off centered."[9]

He went on to explain that he'd depicted the woman's fall with one arm extended out, "because I was hopeful that people would think to grab her, to hold on to her, to connect to the trauma as well as to try to slow the whole thing down a bit."

That's exactly what we'd hoped for, too, in bringing Eric to speak to Canadians and Americans about 9/11 and about his work: that together we could grab on to art as a way to deal with our trauma and pain, and ultimately, to heal.

After leaving the National Gallery, *Tumbling Woman* was displayed for a month in the heart of the embassy, in the center atrium. The night the statue arrived there, Bruce received a call from his assistant telling him that some people were very upset. Some embassy employees had actually chosen diplomatic careers as a personal response to 9/11, a way to give back, and they were disturbed by this work. One woman lost her brother in the aftermath of that tragic day. He'd been a firefighter who was a first responder. He died a few years after 9/11 as a result of lung failure due to smoke inhalation.

"Sir, I think you should consider covering the sculpture," Bruce's assistant said.

"I'm not going to do that," Bruce replied. He was adamant about that, but he did agree to address the issue in two ways. First, he met with the woman who so painfully had lost her brother. She shared her family's story. She told him all about her brave brother, a man who had chosen a profession to serve others; a man who put the call of duty before himself. "I teared up," Bruce told me after. "What she had to say was so moving, so powerful. I'm so grateful to have had a chance to hear her story."

He listened to her point of view. And she listened to him. And after their talk, an amazing thing happened: she changed her mind. She became the most outspoken, positive advocate for why Eric's piece needed to be seen. In the end, she felt that while she had lost a loved one, this sculpture had opened up a conversation that was cathartic for her. She'd been able to express how she felt, and she'd been heard. And because of that, she saw the value of dialogue and wanted it to continue.

Beyond talking to this woman, Bruce also opted to hold an embassy meeting to discuss *Tumbling Woman*. It was held right in front of the statue. There he talked about the importance of sharing our stories and how art can help us do just that. The conversation was opened, and it continued. All who gathered there came with open ears and minds. And the results were incredible.

Later, we hosted a reception for the 9/11 Memorial and Museum at ground zero in Lower Manhattan. We invited the diplomatic corps and many members of the Canadian government. I thanked all the diplomats for their country's support and friendship of the USA in our time of need. There were personal reflections by the numerous diplomats representing countries across the world. The woman who'd lost her brother was there with us that day. She told her family's story of loss and sacrifice to all who would listen. There were tears. There was pain. And there was also healing.

As for Eric Fischl's discussions at the National Gallery, these, too, were a great success. The place was packed, with more than four hundred seats snapped up within days of the event being announced; the waiting list was likewise four hundred strong. Eric was interviewed by gallery director Marc Mayer. He contextualized the piece and spoke about the pain of 9/11 for all of the survivors. The audience heard Eric, and he heard them. We commemorated those who'd been lost, and we shared a moment of mourning and grief.

Tumbling Woman continued to fall, but she reached out to us. And we took her hand. After this exhibition, the bronze version of the statue was displayed in New York City in a show commemorating the fifteenth anniversary of 9/11. Now she can be seen and appreciated in her permanent home at the Whitney Museum of American Art, in Lower Manhattan.

Bruce interviewed Eric at the National Gallery of Canada about the inspiration behind his sculpture.

Stephen Wilkes's visit was the last of the 2015 Contemporary Conversations series and our first by a photographer. Stephen is a charismatic New Yorker, and I knew he would be a hit in Ottawa.

The night before his lecture, we invited eighty young leaders from the Ottawa community to have a conversation at the embassy about the power of documentary photography. These were non-artists—political types who we hoped would be encouraged to think about how to use photography in their political work. Stephen talked with students and political staffers about the power of photography to tell stories and how photographs serve as documents of problems and opportunities in society. He shared his images of Ellis Island and Hurricane Sandy, which wreaked havoc throughout the New York–New Jersey area in 2012 . His photos of Ellis Island had helped secure funding for the restoration of the site, while his photos of Hurricane Sandy brought increased awareness of the impact of climate change. Bruce interviewed him and discussed *Corridor #9, Island 3, Ellis Island* at the National Gallery. As they say, a picture is worth a thousand words.

Ellis Island, located in the bay separating New York City and New Jersey, is where some twelve million immigrants landed from 1892 to 1954 and were processed to become American citizens. Those deemed too ill—either mentally or physically—never left the island. As Wilkes says, "The huddled masses . . . remained huddled—just inches short of the Promised Land." Wilkes shot down a long corridor of what was the infectious disease and psychiatric hospital wings—now overgrown with ivy and vines.

This photograph was a game changer for Stephen. As he told Bruce, "There was history in these walls, these rooms—a very much forgotten history. I discovered I could take photos that had intrinsic beauty but that had a subtext. . . . It made me realize my work could actually create social change. . . . I could bring things that were part of my social consciousness and share those with others."

This was a sentiment I connected with immediately, and so did all of those lucky enough to meet Stephen while he was in Canada. His work went over so well that we arranged for him to return in 2017 to photograph Canada's 150th birthday using his panoramic time-lapse photography technique to capture a single scene's events: the twenty hours of celebration at Parliament Hill on July 1. Bruce and I were in attendance that day. Bruce saw Stephen taking photographs and gave a huge two-armed wave in his direction.

Wouldn't you know it: Stephen managed to capture thousands of people in the crowd that day to create the iconic commemorative photo called *Canada 150*. And Bruce appears in that photo: a little blue pinprick in the crowd, waving his hands up and down like a madman.

Here is Bruce in his blue poncho on Canada Day 2017. Thank you, Stephen Wilkes.

Bees pollinate flowers. Artists pollinate ideas. That first year, I brought great artists to Canada, and the year after, I brought bees to hives in Lornado. The artists came thanks to Art in Embassies, U.S. Embassy Ottawa, and the National Gallery. The bees came thanks to Ted Norris, a beekeeper from Kemptville, south of Ottawa. Ted and I happened to sit next to each other at an event in Toronto in late 2015. The topic of the event was "urban aboriginals"—Ted is Métis and a wonderful mix of urban and rural. I struck up conversation with him and learned that he is passionate about bees and beekeeping.

"I know that bees are seriously under threat. Is it as dire as it seems?" I asked.

"I'm afraid so," he said. "And it's not only bees that face that threat, but the entire ecosystem they support. Without them, flowers can't be pollinated. Without them, crops wouldn't grow."

That was food for thought. It gave me an idea. "Did you know that the White House and the U.S. State Department have made a commit ment to bees?"

Ted looked at me a little skeptically. "What do you mean?"

"The National Pollinator Strategy is a White House plan to increase pollinator-friendly habitat in the United States and at overseas diplomatic posts. Do you know what that means?" I asked.

Ted shook his head.

"It means I need you to bring bees to Ottawa. Ted, would you help? I've got a garden at Lornado that has lots of flowers and could use more pollinators. While I'm no expert, I'm willing to learn if you're willing to teach."

By the time the event was winding down, Ted had agreed to help bring bees to Lornado, and I went home with one of the precious jars of honey he'd brought with him that day.

In the late spring of 2016, Bruce and I trekked out to Ted and Donna's Zen Bee Farm. Ted and his wife, Donna, had started an entire colony for

Ted Norris tending our bees at Lornado.

us to bring to Lornado. We were so excited to learn how to tend them. We dressed in full protective clothing and nervously approached the hives. Ted showed us how to smoke the bees with burning sweetgrass and sage to quiet them down. With his help, we lifted the comb-laden hive panels and held them gingerly in our hands. They were dripping with honey.

"Did you know that bees use magnetism to find their way back home?" Ted told us. "They may venture out into the world, but they always return to their home."

After our beekeeping lesson, Ted and Donna invited us to their home, where they served us mead and bannock, an Indigenous flatbread that was slathered in delicious honey. It was the sweetest meal in every sense—sweet company and sweet delicacies. We sat on their porch and absorbed everything we could about the craft of beekeeping.

We saw Ted again when he delivered a hundred thousand bees to Lornado. The hives, surrounded by a picket fence, looked like miniature white houses with pitched roofs. Under his guidance, I purchased two sets of beekeeper's gear: ventilated suits (embroidered with the Lornado logo; I called them the Ghostbuster suits), veils, and long protective gloves. These outfits meant that embassy staff and I could tend to the bees. It also meant we could one day harvest the honey they would produce.

Ted taught me and the staff all about hive bodies (the boxes that house the bees), frames (where the bees create the honeycomb), smokers (harmless devices used to calm agitated bees), and about uncapping knives (used to remove the wax that the bees use to keep the honey from absorbing water). He taught us that a hive is always presided over by a queen bee. A single queen mothers as many as fifty thousand bees in her hive. Without the queen, there is no honey. Without the queen, there is no hive.

"Do you think we'll get any honey this year?" I asked Ted before he left that day.

Here I am being outfitted in beekeeper's gear with the help of Ted Norris. We are ready to get to work.

"We'll get some," he said. "But it's hard to know how much. It's just the first year. It takes time for bees to set up a thriving and productive hive and to collect enough nectar to make honey."

Of course. That made a lot of sense. It's how I felt about my work during that first year in Ottawa. It took time and diligence, hard work and patience to make our hive successful. The honey was yet to come.

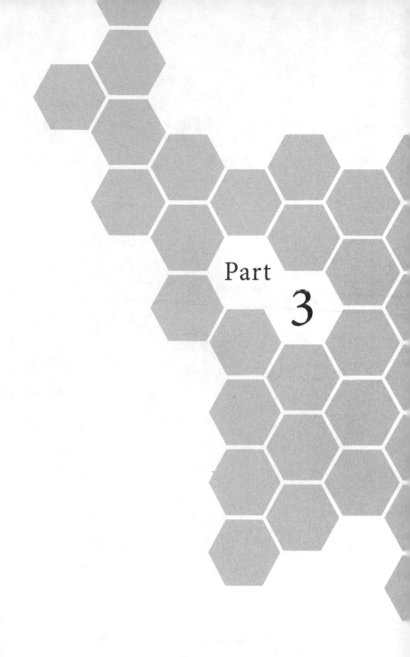

Part

3

Chapter 8

The Way You Make Your Bed

Bruce

My father, Miles Heyman, was a traveling salesman, as was his father. A born entrepreneur, he was selling magazines out of a wagon at the age of five, and, by thirteen, he had launched his own lawn-cutting business.

I learned a lot from my father, and I still hear his voice in my head repeating the many maxims he taught me from an early age:

"Engage your brain before putting your mouth into gear."

"Don't let the bully take you down."

"The way you make your bed is the way you lie in it."

Another lesson I learned from my father was to listen carefully, not just to the most senior person in the ranks but also, just as importantly, to the most junior. This was something my father probably learned on the road after countless sales calls: that it was the "ordinary people on the street" who often had the most wisdom, vision, and intuition about business and about life. And yet these people were rarely in charge of the decision-making that would make an impact.

My father died in 2012, when I was fifty-four years old. Isn't it funny how no matter your age, you still want to do right by your parents? My father was someone who made time for everyone, no matter his or her rank or salary, and I aim to follow in his footsteps. When I was at Goldman Sachs, my father was there for me with advice anytime—always just a phone call away. And after he passed away, while he was no longer with me in person, his spirit remained close to my heart. It remains close to my heart to this day.

One of the things I did early on at Goldman was to promote a flat structure, where power is not always hierarchical. This was Goldman culture, and it's what I took to Ottawa. I also made friends with people doing every kind of job in the building, including my good friend Yvonne Randle, who is a long-serving security guard in the building on South Wacker Drive where the Goldman Sachs Chicago office is located. Yvonne is the embodiment of happiness. She always has the biggest smile. She would regale me with stories about her beloved granddaughter and how proud she was of her. When the markets were tumultuous, or when I was navigating personnel challenges at work, Yvonne provided my daily dose of optimism. On March 9, 2009—my birthday—the market was crashing, and we were rapidly entering a financial crisis.

"Bruce, today's your birthday," she said. "Don't worry. Things are going to take a turn for the better. That will be your birthday gift!"

Wouldn't you know it: Yvonne was right. That day was the exact bottom of the market; everything got better after that.

Yvonne was so important to me—such a valued figure in my life—that when I became ambassador, I called her up and said, "Yvonne, it's Bruce. Guess what?"

"What?"

"I got a new job. I've been named U.S. ambassador to Canada. There's going to be a swearing-in ceremony in Washington. Would you come?"

I think I surprised her just a little with that. "Well, I'd be honored." Yvonne was right there at the State Department in Washington, DC, with all my friends and family during my swearing-in on March 26, 2014.

I know that in a lot of organizations not everyone feels empowered to express his or her point of view or to build collegial relationships that aren't about rank and hierarchy. Some employees are afraid to "tell it like it is" because perhaps their superiors will not like what they have to say, or maybe they'll be branded as "troublemakers" or "climbers." I have learned throughout my career that the so-called rank and file can sometimes pinpoint problems better—if they are empowered with the freedom to share their observations. By listening closely, I develop a deeper understanding of who does what, where there are gaps and inefficiencies, and which staff members are making important—though sometimes overlooked—contributions to the company. In life, as in business, there's the 80–20 rule: 20 percent of the people do 80 percent of the work. News flash: it isn't always the most senior people who are doing the most work.

When I began in my posting as ambassador, one of the first things I did at the embassy was get a lunch program up and running. How did it work? Simple: I told my assistant, "Book me lunches. Only rules? I pay, and no senior staff."

"But, Mr. Ambassador, if you ask employees to a private lunch, they may think they're getting fired."

"Fired? No! People are getting *fries.* Maybe a sandwich and a drink, too. I just want to hear from people individually about what challenges they face in their jobs. I want to help all of us work better together."

For some of the embassy staff, this way of operating posed a big adjustment. There were people who'd worked in government for more than twenty years and had never once had a conversation with an ambassador, never mind a meal. How is that possible?

I remember one lunch with a very smart woman who worked in a management position at the embassy. She pointed out some areas where we needed to make improvements to be more efficient and effective.

"You know," I said, "I'm really glad you told me this. And if you see something that I could be doing better or something we can fix, will you just call me in the future?"

She put down her fork and went for her water glass. She took a gulp and swallowed. Then she said, "No, sir. There's zero chance of me calling you. I hope you understand that doing so would put my career at risk."

I was stunned by her response, but I also understood her justified fears. She was worried that her superiors would see this as "going over their heads" and that it could limit her career prospects—or worse. What this showed me was that I had a lot of work to do to improve the culture in the embassy.

I made a point of changing the dynamic, of empowering junior people to feel free to speak up the same way I'd done at Goldman Sachs. When I booked meetings, I'd ask senior staff to bring certain juniors to high-level discussions.

"I'm sorry, what? We don't need my junior person at this meeting. I have all their information because they report to me."

"That's great!" I'd say. "So since your junior did all the work, let's have him or her present at the meeting. It'll be fantastic. You and I can sit back, listen, and learn. Plus, your staff will have a chance to shine."

Sometimes this approach went over well, sometimes it didn't. It was a culture shift, that's for sure.

"You're a disruptor," Vicki said when I told her what I was up to.

"You make it sound like a bad thing," I replied.

"Oh, no, it's not bad. You're a *positive* disruptive force. But you're a force all the same," she said, smiling.

In July 2015 I put my disruptive tendencies on hold to go to Vancouver, where I would greet Vice President Joe Biden at the airport, alongside his wife, Jill, and three of his grandchildren, as well as Michelle and Barack

Welcoming Vice President Biden, Dr. Jill Biden, their grandchildren, and Sasha Obama, who were in Vancouver to watch the United States Women's National Soccer team play Japan for the World Cup.

Obama's younger daughter, Sasha. When they landed, the mood of well-wishers at the airport was buoyant. The crowd chanted, "USA! USA!"

And yet these were troubling times for the vice president. His elder son, Beau Biden—the attorney general of Delaware—had died of a brain tumor in May. Joe had come with his grandkids to cheer on the American women's soccer team, which was playing against Japan for the World Cup. He and Jill had just lost their son. His grandkids had just lost their father. At the same time, there was a political agenda for the trip. Biden was scheduled to meet with Prime Minister Harper to talk about security issues, the economy, and the ongoing threat posed by ISIS.

I had a private moment with Joe while we were in the skybox watching the game.

"Joe," I said, "I can't even begin to imagine your pain right now. And I want you to know that I'm here for you, whatever you need."

He had a stoic look about him, but I could see the grief in the set of his shoulders and in his eyes.

"I appreciate that, Bruce," he said. He was forthright about the pain he was in over the loss of his son, and we spoke about that for a while. I told him that I was confident that many of us who worked on the Obama campaigns would support him if he decided to run in the next election. "The country would benefit from your leadership and experience," I said.

He ended up not running, and I sometimes wonder where we would be today if things had been different and his son hadn't been taken away from him so soon.

"Looks like things are going our way in this game," I said as I eyed the scoreboard. The United States was well in the lead against Japan. Joe and I left the box and joined Jill and the kids in the stands to watch the rest of the game. In the end, we won 5–2.

"Let's get down there and celebrate," Joe said, and so we did. We all went down to the field to congratulate the team. It was so great to see a bit of joy on Joe's grandkids' faces.

"We won, we won!" they said over and over again.

"Yes, isn't it fantastic?" Joe said. I don't know how he found the strength to be so positive and enthusiastic while in a state of grief, but that's what makes him such an extraordinary man: he's able to rise above whatever he feels in the moment and be there for others.

As for the meeting with Harper, Joe conducted himself in exactly the same way as always. He was friendly, personable, professional. He reminded me then of my father. Always kind, always there for others, even at the worst of times, always prepared. *The way you make your bed is the way you lie in it.*

The prime minister began by expressing his condolences to the vice president.

The vice president thanked him.

Then both of them got to work.

Within the embassy, I worked hard to make things less hierarchical. I wanted to open up the lines of communication and facilitate information flow between departments. I mirrored this approach in my diplomatic work between Canada and the United States as well. When it came time to address a major issue such as trade, for instance, I wanted to learn first what was working and then how to build upon that success—and not just for the United States but also for the good of Canada. I didn't care if a U.S. company opened a plant on the Canadian side of the border or vice versa. Instead of tit for tat, what I wanted to encourage was more trade in general. We needed more people hired for more jobs, be they talented and qualified Canadians or talented and qualified Americans. I wanted people to be gainfully employed, because if the economy flourished, so would citizens in both of our countries.

As ambassador, whenever I talked about Canadians coming to America to open businesses, I said, "I don't want to take your company, I want you to expand it. And when you're ready to expand, choose the

USA. Pick *our* country, and let me help you do that. Let me make it an easy choice."

When barriers existed, I'd ask the U.S. Department of Commerce to wade through the myriad rules and regulations. In a way, I saw my role as being the cheerleader of cross-border business, which is so different from the tone that is currently being set by Trump and his administration.

I was outcome oriented when it came to business and trade opportunities, and I was outcome oriented in the political realm as well. Often I'd be informed by the embassy staff that we were going to take a meeting with a certain minister.

"Great," I'd say. "What for?"

"What do you mean, *What for?*" they'd ask. "To build a relationship, of course."

There's nothing wrong with meetings to build relationships, but when you have only so many opportunities to meet high-level ministers or whatever VIP applies in your field, it's best to use the opportunity to further a goal. And what if no goal has been articulated? Well, then it's time to take a step back and do some advanced planning and strategic thinking to put a goal in place.

That's the position I found myself in during the summer of 2015. The federal election in Canada was slated for the end of October, so we had time for some advance planning. I asked the embassy to write a "position paper" outlining the three scenarios of government that could occur in the fall and what our agendas and priorities would be depending on who was elected: Stephen Harper for another term, Justin Trudeau, or Tom Mulcair, the leader of the New Democratic Party of Canada. I asked each department head at the embassy to work with his or her colleagues in Washington to develop a set of goals and a blueprint for achievement. We would then present the results to each other in our weekly embassy "country team" meeting.

Some people balked at this idea, and some people really buckled down to get the work done. I assigned deadlines, and I put one person in charge of consolidating and sharing information.

Every department of the U.S. embassy prepared a position paper and then presented it to every other department. The results? While the priorities shifted somewhat depending on who was elected, what was more important was how the exercise forced everyone to know all three political landscapes and to set goals for all three possible political outcomes. Also, departments had to talk to one another and work together. If Homeland Security wanted to implement changes at the border, that might impact trade, at which point the Department of Commerce would need to be involved. All groups needed to understand the issues at play.

The exercise was a great success, so much so that we decided to turn the findings into the blueprint for the relationship between Canada and the United States during the balance of my tenure. Next, I conducted an equivalent meeting in Washington with representatives from every government agency and White House representation too. We convened in a large conference room. It was amazing. All of these departments and agencies were working and strategizing together, and suddenly this enlarged "country team" in Washington had a 360-degree perspective on so many issues and on how to tackle them in the future, no matter who was in power. I walked through all three scenarios with the entire team. When I got to the scenario of Trudeau winning, I remember saying, "Based on his campaign promises, Trudeau's agenda lines up most directly with that of the Obama administration. If he wins, we're going to be in a position to do a lot of great work."

"Do you think he can win?" I was asked.

"I have no idea," I said. "We're here to investigate potential outcomes, not to place bets."

Back in Ottawa, Vicki and I couldn't help but hear opinions and thoughts about the upcoming election from Canadians. I'd grown close to several of our RCMP officers, and they'd share with me what they'd seen during rallies and campaign meetings, since a few of them had served as security.

"Trudeau's crowds are large," one told me. "People stand in line for hours to talk to him. Mulcair's events are a bit easier on us as security. Not so many people to keep watch over."

"I see," I said.

"How are Harper's events?"

"Not sure. I haven't been assigned to his detail."

Vicki and I would talk about the election, what was different in Canada, and what was the same as our experiences in the United States. Vicki has participated in politics long enough to know that being an underdog and being scrappy can, in some circumstances, be a distinct advantage.

"What do you think?" I asked her. "Can Trudeau do this?"

"Bruce, you already know my answer."

And I did. Yes. He. Can.

The day of the election, I asked those gathered in the embassy, "Who here thinks Trudeau will win?" Not a single person raised a hand. I waited a moment and then raised my hand.

Silence.

"Well, that's what I think," I said with a shrug. "I think he's got a chance. But I'm not voting—I guess we'll see the results tonight."

On election night, October 19, 2015, we stayed home at Lornado. Vicki and I had dinner in front of the TV. The red Liberal Party wave started on the East Coast, but it didn't stop there. Once it passed Quebec and then spread through Ontario, we knew that Trudeau had won.

Vicki could not help herself. "He told you all along," she said, a little twinkle in her eye. "He's got this."

The day after Trudeau's victory, she went to Sophie and Justin's home in Rockcliffe and knocked on the front door. It opened, and there stood

Sophie. Just inside was her mother, Estelle Blais, and little Hadrien, who was then just twenty months old.

"Congratulations, *mon amie*!" Vicki exclaimed, and the two shared a teary hug.

"How are you feeling?" Vicki asked.

"I am so happy," she said. "This is such a big responsibility, but we can do this."

You can imagine what Vicki said next. Then she passed Sophie a box.

"What is this?"

"It's the American flag," Vicki said. "This is the flag that we flew over the U.S. embassy yesterday, on Election Day, when voters across your country chose Justin as their prime minister. I want you to have this as a symbol of our friendship and of the great things that the United States and Canada can do together."

Sophie was touched by this gesture.

The day after Trudeau's swearing-in, which took place just two and a half weeks later, Vicki asked our chef, Dino, to bake up some cookies with both the maple leaf and the American flag. She had them wrapped up and delivered to every elected cabinet minister sworn in. She hand delivered some herself, giving those she knew big hugs and offering her congratulations.

Leave it to my wife to think of everything and to mark the moment in such a special, human way.

Chapter 9

Grace Will Lead Us Home

Vicki

There were the Harper months, and there were the Trudeau months—and they were as different as night and day. The Trudeau months were warm, invigorating, and youthful from the moment Justin stepped into power as the twenty-third prime minister of Canada. From our point of view, the change could not have been more dramatic—and, given how much the media were commenting on this new era of change, many Canadians shared our opinion. Trudeau's style of leadership stood out in such sharp contrast with Harper's. He was open and inviting; he was inclusive. Right from the beginning of his term, he was set on modernizing and innovating how things were done, both in government and in Canada at large.

Before winning the election, Trudeau promised that his cabinet would be different from any that Canadians had seen in the past. And post-election, what's the first thing he did? He kept his promise. He chose fifteen women for his cabinet, for a total of 50 percent representation. When he was asked why parity was important, he replied bluntly, "Because it's 2015."

Trudeau's government was officially sworn in on November 4, 2015, a cool, crisp, bluebird day in Ottawa. The leaves were changing as the swearing-in took place at Rideau Hall. The road was lined with happy Canadians, cheering and clapping. And that cabinet—it was full of vibrant, diverse people who reflected contemporary Canada. There was such animation and euphoria that day. Bruce attended the swearing-in ceremony. Later, I asked him, "Being up close like that, was it as momentous as the media made it seem?"

"More, Vicki," he said. "More."

That's what I expected he'd say, and his response made me very happy.

Not long after that, Trudeau was off to Paris for the COP21, the Conference of the Parties to the UN Framework Convention on Climate Change (UNFCCC), which was the twenty-first conference gathering more than 150 nations to discuss a possible new global agreement on combatting climate change. This conference would later lead to the signing of the Paris Agreement in mid-2016, when, under Prime Minister Trudeau's leadership, the Canadian government, alongside the United States, committed to reducing greenhouse gas emissions by 30 percent more than the previous goal set by the Conservative Canadian government.

Trudeau addressed the COP21 in Paris. "My message is simple," he said. "Canada can and will do more to address the global challenge of climate change." He closed by saying, "Canada is back, my good friends. We are here to help. To build an agreement that will do our children and our grandchildren proud."

This was one of many massive and substantive changes that marked right away what would be different under Trudeau's leadership. And when the winter holiday season rolled around a few weeks later, more changes were apparent to Bruce and to me. During our time in Ottawa up to then, we had never been to any event where the prime minister had personally welcomed foreign dignitaries and ambassadors. But in December Prime Minister Trudeau invited every diplomat living in Ottawa to Parliament for holiday celebrations. There were probably more than five hundred people there that evening. The halls were truly decked for the occasion, too. Every time we'd been to Parliament previously, the corridors were sober and hallowed, quiet and formal. But on this occasion, the halls were decorated in garlands and lights, and filled with holiday cheer. There was Canadian music and delicious Canadian food.

"Do you recognize this place?" Bruce asked me at some point during the evening.

"It's a little different," I said as I took in the groups of people around us engaged in animated conversation, drinks in hand.

Justin and Sophie created a receiving line in the library of Parliament. It's a stunning room full of precious volumes and historical books, and the only room to have survived a fire that razed the building in 1916. There they personally greeted every single guest, including Bruce and me. Both were aware of which countries guests represented and directed their conversations accordingly. They made a point of saying they wanted to stay in contact and to hear from everyone there.

"Bruce, Vicki! It's so lovely to see you!" Justin said when we made our way to the front of the receiving line. Both he and Sophie threw their arms open to us. It was like a string of lights had just been switched on, from darkness to light.

The next night, we hosted a holiday party at the ambassador's residence. The whole time we'd been in Ottawa, Prime Minister Harper had never been to Lornado, but Trudeau and many of his new cabinet ministers arrived at our door to ring in the holidays. It was a surprise to our guests, and the entire house was filled with excitement at the arrival of their new prime minister.

Not too long after that, Sophie and Justin invited us to Harrington

The newly elected prime minister of Canada attended our annual Lornado holiday party in 2015. It was a wonderful surprise for our guests.

Lake—the ministerial retreat, and the Canadian equivalent of Camp David, the presidential retreat in Maryland—for a family day with their children and Sophie's parents. By this point, our two families had become quite close, and we could enjoy each other's company without having to discuss politics to any great degree. I recall telling them both about our children—David, Liza, and Caroline—and about our three darling grandchildren. They conversed freely with us about their own families, their childhood experiences, and all the exciting possibilities ahead. We knew this property, just northwest of Ottawa, was such an important place for Justin. He'd spent so many wonderful years there with his father, Pierre, and mother, Margaret.

Sophie prepared a lovely brunch that day, after which we all donned snowshoes and went out for a walk in the woods. Justin helped me navigate fallen trees on a steep hillside. He took my hand and steadied my steps as we tracked through the snow.

From time to time, my husband gets this very particular look on his face. It's his "lost in thought" look. I saw this expression appear on his face at Harrington Lake.

"What are you thinking about?" I asked.

"Can you imagine," Bruce said, "all of the prime ministers and guests, all of the conversations that must have taken place on this property?"

Indeed. So much history and lore in one place. As Bruce and I tried to keep pace with Justin and Sophie, who are incredible athletes and were much more adept with snowshoes than we were, Justin shared with us some of his fond memories from the years he spent with his family at Harrington Lake when he was just a child. I could see his "lost in thought" look, too, as he remembered happy times.

Sophie told me all about the gardens, which were buried beneath the snow. She talked about how much she enjoyed the lake in the summer. I envisioned the whole family in canoes. Her mother-in-law, Margaret Trudeau, had added a vegetable plot to the property when she was living there in the 1970s. Apparently, somewhere underneath the snowbanks, the garden was dormant, just waiting for temperatures to warm. Sophie was excited to see what would come up in the spring.

"You must be excited, too," she said. "To see what comes up in Lornado's garden next spring."

"I am," I said. "Isn't it incredible how so much change can occur in just one year; so much growth and new life?"

I was talking about the gardens, but I meant much more than that, too.

In March 2016, I continued the Contemporary Conversations series. The first year was a proven success, and the State Department had noticed.

"It's good," they as much as said. They couldn't help but notice the long, enthusiastic articles in *Ottawa Citizen*, *The Globe and Mail*, and the Canadian magazine *The Walrus*. This had raised our profile, and we were eager to do more in our sophomore year. Fortunately, we received more funding, which meant we really could expand our footprint beyond Ottawa.

The first artist we brought to Ottawa in 2016 was Kiki Smith, one of the most hardworking, provocative American artists of her generation. A feminist and a maverick, she fit very well within our mandate to promote artists who were opening up conversations about identity. At the National Gallery, she revealed an awe-inspiring bronze sculpture she called *Born*, which depicts a fully formed woman being born from a deer. Like many artists, Kiki resists defining and explaining her work. Rather, her motive is to present it and let viewers make what they will of it. "I always liked the idea of making things that are really open, that everybody can come to with their own ideas and responses," she has explained.[1]

The natural world features prominently in Kiki's work and in her life's work as well. When she came to Lornado and saw our gardens, she said, "Did you know I'm a beekeeper too?"

"What? I did not!" I said, though it is so in keeping with Kiki's curiosity and love for the natural world that I should hardly have been surprised. In an interview about her art, Kiki once said that she felt the

Multidisciplinary artist Kiki Smith in front of the National Gallery in Ottawa.

fate of humankind was intimately connected with the health of the environment. And somehow, when I look at her art, that's what I see: a plea for us to listen closely and to preserve the mystery and enchantment that the natural world offers as its gifts to us.

Kiki is herself an artist born of artists. Her mother was an opera singer, and her father was the much-lauded Anthony Peter Smith, American sculptor, visual artist, and architectural designer. While Kiki's talk broke National Gallery attendance records, what stands out most for me is the moment when she saw how her work was featured in the gallery alongside her father's. When she walked into that room, she was taken aback. One of the first things she saw was some old video footage of herself, her father, and her sisters at home together making art. Throughout the room were letters and other memorabilia that for any student of art would have been a fascinating representation of how art travels through generations, how it passes from hand to hand, from parents to children. But for Kiki, it was deeply personal. These were her father's hands and her sisters' hands—and her own.

I asked her how she felt. She was very moved and overwhelmed. Her father had died more than three decades before, but the installation had brought him back to vivid life before her eyes—and as an artist, her work was paired with his for what may have been the very first time. I was proud and pleased to have helped commemorate not just one but two brilliant artists in this powerful way.

Later that year, we brought Theaster Gates to Canada, which I was incredibly excited about, since I'd admired his work for so many years. Theaster is a painter, sculptor, performance artist, singer, chef, academic, speaker, potter, and truly a civic treasure of my hometown, Chicago. Beyond his work in the arts, he is also an incredible community advocate. The Rebuild Foundation, which he founded, is a platform for art, cultural development, and neighborhood transformation on the South Side of Chicago.

I could not wait for Ottawa to hear Theaster's stories and to see his art, which addresses social justice, race, identity, and self-discovery. One of his signature pieces, called *Ole Spangled Banner*, was on display at Lornado as part of the Art in Embassies program. Using old fire hoses, like those turned on peaceful protesters during the civil rights struggles of the sixties, Theaster created a flag-like tapestry that evokes the iconic stripes and color scheme of the American flag. When you look at the piece, you're compelled to revisit those civil rights demonstrations and to remember how those hoses were used in such a violent way against peaceful citizens.

Theaster's visit to Ottawa included an onstage interview and Q&A at the National Gallery. He talked about race and social justice. He told story after story about how his art and work have inspired and affected social change around the world. Theaster received the first standing ovation of the series. Afterward, he was the guest of honor for a dinner we hosted at Lornado. We cleared the living room to make space for forty-eight guests. The guest list was one of the most eclectic we'd ever assembled, encompassing a cross section of Canadian and American political leaders, artists, dancers, performers, clothing designers, and academics. Attendees included Ming Tiampo, a dear friend and professor of art history; graffiti artist Allan André; Canada's finance minister, Bill Morneau; Alberta artist Chris Cran; social entrepreneur Gabriel Lopez; and photographer-activist David Pistol. We also invited Séan McCann, the former singer with the popular Newfoundland folk-rock band Great Big Sea. I'd met him two months earlier when he spoke and performed at a benefit for the Ottawa Youth Services Bureau. Séan's songs, written about his struggles with addiction and about sexual abuse he'd experienced as a child, moved me. I wanted to know him better and include him with the other powerful artists and storytellers that we were bringing to Lornado. I asked him in advance if he would mind bringing his acoustic guitar, which he calls Old Brown, and he was kind enough to oblige.

As dinner came to an end on the night of the event, Séan winked at me and said, "Should I get Old Brown out now?"

Theaster Gates standing with Bruce and me in front of his piece *Ole Spangled Banner* at Lornado.

"That would be so lovely," I replied.

Séan sang a beautiful song, and as he finished, Theaster broke out into "Amazing Grace." I couldn't believe my ears: this was a meaningful choice for Theaster, since the National Gallery had acquired a video he made called "Billy Sings Amazing Grace." In the video, Theaster's group of singers, the Monks of Mississippi, sings a rendition of the spiritual hymn with Billy, an elderly man from the housing projects in Houston. For Theaster to choose that song and to offer it up for all gathered there to listen—this was a gift.

> *Amazing Grace, how sweet the sound*
> *That saved a wretch like me*

At some point, Séan began to strum sweetly behind Theaster's melody. The barest of chords lifted his voice even higher.

> *Through many pains and toils and snares*
> *I have already come.*

As the hymn continued, Séan added his voice to Theaster's as accompaniment. Not only was practically every guest at that table moved to tears by the impromptu duet, we were also bearing witness to a moment we would never forget. I watched as Lornado staff came through the threshold with platters and serving dishes only to be instantly struck still and silent by the spectacle. They watched as Theaster led the hymn to its powerful close:

> *'Twas your grace that brought us safe thus far*
> *And grace will lead me home.*

Amen to that.

Chapter 10

When the Walls Come Tumbling Down

Bruce

Following the terrorist attacks of 9/11, the U.S. embassy in Ottawa changed a great deal, as did so much of North America and the world. National security became top of mind, and as such, it was decided that more needed to be done to protect the entrance of all American embassies. At the U.S. embassy in Ottawa, large cement barriers were constructed to prevent anyone from using a vehicle to make a direct attack on the building. This, the staff was told at the time, would be a temporary measure. Eventually the obstructions would be torn down. But thirteen years later, when my tenure began, those barriers remained.

That's the danger of walls: when they go up, we get used to them. They become just another obstacle we have to find our way around. It's easy to forget what it was like before that barrier existed. And, worse still, we eventually forget what it was like to live in a world without any walls at all.

Upon my arrival in Ottawa, I could immediately see the impact the cement barriers were having on the entranceway to the embassy. The first impression visitors received was one of authority and defensiveness, coupled with a vague sense of foreboding. It made me think back to Robert Frost and his well-known poem "Mending Wall." Some people didn't know what the big deal was when I brought up the issue. I paraphrased Frost as my answer. "When you construct a barrier," I said, "you need to think about who you're walling in and who you're walling out. And to whom you're likely to give offense."

My concerns sometimes met with shoulder shrugs. The barriers had become part of the landscape—a backdrop of obstruction.

Before Canada's 150th celebration, I met with Mark Kristmanson, the head of the National Capital Commission, and with Ottawa mayor Jim Watson. Both were interested in beautifying the capital for the big anniversary. "Don't you think we should get rid of those concrete eyesores?" I asked. "Isn't it time?"

Mark and Jim agreed, but when I shared our ideas with some of the other stakeholders within the embassy, they had concerns about the cost. "There are budget constraints, Ambassador. Are you sure you want to prioritize dismantling security barriers?"

That's exactly what I wanted to do, but I had more homework to do first. My next step was to assemble a team within the embassy, led by our regional security officer, Charlie Brandeis. Given his numerous international postings, he was well briefed in security measures. What would the building look like without those imposing concrete monoliths? What would it cost to tear them down? Would the building be secure without them?

Charlie educated me on all of these matters. "Did you know that bollards put deep in the ground are actually safer than those giant cement things you currently have at the embassy?" he explained. "If a truck hits a cement barrier at a hundred fifty kilometers per hour, it'll push that cement right in. But bollards? Bollards won't move." Bollards, I came to learn, are short, sturdy vertical posts made of steel.

Food for thought. I called Mayor Watson. "How would we get this completed if we were able to find a way forward?"

"It's simple," he said. "You get funding from the Capital Commission and the U.S. government, and the city of Ottawa will join in. We'll contract for the removal of the cement barriers and any other related construction work." Excellent. The mayor was on board.

I went back to the Capital Commission, which eventually gave me the all clear. My next step was to present my plan to Washington. I flew there to meet with people at the U.S. State Department. As I walked into the meeting room, I couldn't help but notice all the photos of American embassies on the walls. Ours was depicted, too: a beautiful photo of it before the barriers had been erected.

I asked a staff member for a favor. "Listen, I'm about to go into a meeting, and I need this picture. Can you take it down from the wall and bring it to my meeting room?"

Having started in the middle of my story, I understandably received a puzzled look. I backed up and explained that, contrary to appearances, I was not an art thief but a U.S. ambassador presenting an embassy renovation plan to the Washington team.

The man agreed to help out rather than call security. Before the meeting began, the photo was placed at the end of the boardroom table so that everyone in the room could view it.

I made my presentation to about twenty-five people. I referenced the photo of the embassy from their hallway, which showed so clearly what the building had looked like before the barriers were constructed. Everyone agreed that it was beautiful. Next, I showed them a photo of what the embassy looked like now.

"Oh," they said, "that's really an eyesore."

A picture is worth a thousand words, as they say.

I went on to discuss the need to work with Ottawa for its 150th celebration and to transform the fortified entrance into a bike lane—beautification, security, partnership, and promotion of bike use in the capital city of Canada. I shared my financial plan to make the changes happen.

"This all makes sense," I was told. "Go make it happen."

So I did.

The result? The embassy doesn't look like a forbidding fortress anymore. It was restored as the inviting front door of our country. And not only is security now enhanced, but also dozens of cyclists use the path at the front of the embassy every single day.

As soon as those obstructions were gone, the response we received from the staff and the public was extremely positive.

"This is so much better!" they said.

"It feels so much more hospitable and open now."

"I feel good when I come in here."

And isn't that the way it is when the walls come tumbling down?

You feel good.

You feel welcomed.

You feel at home.

I worked with the city of Ottawa to transform the fortified entrance of the embassy into a more welcoming space by adding bike lanes.

It wasn't long after Justin Trudeau was sworn in as prime minister that his Principal Secretary, Gerald Butts—Gerry, as he is called—and I discussed a possible meeting in Washington between the prime minister and the president. Little did he know that plans were in the works for a much more significant meeting.

Justin had met Barack Obama previously, and it was obvious to most observers that the two men had a natural connection—a bromance, as it came to be called by the press.

"Gerry," I said. "We'd like to invite the prime minister to a state dinner in Washington. What do you say?"

I'll never forget Gerry's emphatic "*Yes!*" It had been nineteen years since a Canadian prime minister had attended a state dinner, so this was no small thing. (Obama would later remark, just like a Canadian, "About time, eh?")

After Trudeau formally accepted the invitation, the backroom planning began. This was Justin Trudeau's first state dinner as prime minister, and it was my first time being involved in planning one. I learned quickly that a state dinner isn't just a dinner—at least not in the Obama world. It would be the culmination of a set of accomplishments made between Canada and the United States, so that both leaders could announce those accomplishments at the event and celebrate them together in front of the world.

We spent the next three months preparing. Fortunately, all the pre-election groundwork we'd done on goals and priorities meant that we had a comprehensive road map to follow. In the course of preparations, I started to think about how amazing it would be if this weren't an end goal but just the first step in building even better relations between our two nations. At the embassy, every day as I headed to my office, I walked by quotes from four different presidents about the importance of the relationship between the United States and Canada. They served as my daily reminder of what my job was really about—what mattered most.

From Dwight D. Eisenhower: "Here, on this continent, we present an example that other nations some day surely will recognize and apply in their relationships among themselves."

John F. Kennedy: "Geography has made us neighbors. History has made us friends. Economics has made us partners, and necessity has made us allies."

Ronald Reagan: "Let the 5,000-mile border between Canada and the United States stand as a symbol for the future. Let it forever be not a point of division but a meeting place between our great and true friends."

William J. Clinton: "As we stand on the threshold of a new millennium, let us build a future of peace and prosperity, of freedom and dignity for our continent and beyond."

I dreamed about adding a quote from Obama one day. And that led me to a new thought: What if, after Trudeau's state dinner, Obama were to reciprocate with a visit to Canada?

I talked with Gerry. "What do you think of Obama coming here and speaking to Parliament?" I asked, just like that.

"Are you *kidding* me?" he said. "I can't speak for the prime minister right this second, obviously, but we would *highly entertain* such a thing."

So throughout our negotiations for Trudeau's state dinner, we were also looking ahead to a time when Obama might visit Canada. There was a lot of back-and-forth between our representatives; a lot of negotiation about what could and could not happen. Finally, we arrived at an agreement by the president of the United States that if he were asked by the prime minister to visit Canada and speak in Parliament, he would say yes. All that remained to be seen was when and how the "ask" would take place.

Meanwhile, negotiations for the state dinner continued. One of the goals we discussed was a significant expansion of existing pre-clearance screening by U.S. customs agents at select airports, railway stations, and on cruise ships. This would help secure our shared border and ensure a better experience for American and Canadian travelers. We also discussed what remarks would be made at the state dinner and even what gifts might be exchanged. Gerry had a unique idea: he had this vision of giving maple trees to Washington as a gift. He imagined all those trees with their leaves turning a glorious red. What better enduring symbol of Canada could there be? Of course, Washington is known for its spectacular cherry trees, a gift from Japan in 1912. They're a stunning spectacle to behold every spring. I wasn't sure how this notion of a new pageant of trees would go down. I asked Vicki what she thought of the idea.

"I think it would be extraordinary," she said.

We put the idea on the table and hoped it would be well received.

Months of preparation. Months of negotiation right until the last moment. And finally, the three-day visit that included the state dinner arrived. It was March 9, 2016. I was just beginning my third year as U.S. ambassador to Canada. I was involved in planning a state dinner between two world leaders whom I respected highly and knew would accomplish so much together. And beyond that, it was also my birthday. Could a man's fifty-eighth birthday get any better than that?

Out on the vast tarmac at Andrews Air Force Base near Washington, DC, I waited with Vicki and David MacNaughton, the Canadian ambassador to the United States—all of us there to welcome the Airbus A310-300 bringing Prime Minister Justin Trudeau to the United States. The sun was shining. It was a freakishly warm day, with the temperature at a record-setting 80 degrees Fahrenheit (or as Canadians would say, 26 degrees Celsius). Washington's famed cherry trees were in bloom a week ahead of schedule.

"How are you feeling?" Vicki asked me.

"This is the best birthday of my life," I replied.

She gave my hand a squeeze.

The plane landed smoothly and came to a stop. The doors were opened, and as the passengers came down the stairs, I was smiling ear to ear. Down the back stairs came Sophie's parents, Jean Grégoire and Estelle Blais, and Justin's mother, Margaret. Then there was Trudeau's

Vicki and I greet Prime Minister Trudeau and his family as they arrive for their first state visit to the United States.

team, including Gerry Butts; Katie Telford, his chief of staff; Kate Purchase, his communications director; and Mélanie Joly, the Canadian heritage minister. Also included were Paul Wells, a senior writer with *Maclean's* magazine and several other journalists. Down the front stairs came Prime Minister Trudeau and Sophie, along with their three children, Xavier (then eight), Ella-Grace (seven), and Hadrien (two)—all arm in arm. We had developed not just a working relationship with all of these people but also a friendship. For Vicki and me, we weren't just welcoming dignitaries but introducing old friends to new ones.

"Mr. Ambassador, happy birthday to you!" Justin and Sophie said as Vicki and I rushed to give them big hugs.

"Can't think of a better gift than this," I replied.

For both Vicki and me, this was such a high point in our lives and careers. It took us back to 2008 when Obama was first elected. It was like we had seen this movie before. We knew the ending. And it was right around the corner. The lack of cynicism, the vision to work together, the exhilaration, the hope. We couldn't wait for the Canadians to meet the Americans. The fresh faces of the future were coming off the plane that day.

A great deal of pageantry and ceremony mark state visits. But the welcome Trudeau and his team received the following day from the U.S. capital was unlike anything I'd ever seen. There were military bands playing rousing music on the White House lawn, there were receiving lines, there was a review of the troops, honor guards, a nineteen-gun salute. Pennsylvania Avenue was lined with as many Canadian flags as American ones.

After this warm welcome, I went to the Oval Office with the prime minister and the president while Vicki accompanied a small group that went with Sophie and Michelle Obama to a Let Girls Learn event: an initiative, promoted by the First Lady, dedicated to tearing down barriers that prevent adolescent girls all over the world from receiving a quality education.

"Sophie and Michelle connected so beautifully," Vicki told me later. Each woman spoke passionately and purposefully about the importance of giving girls and women an education. They encouraged the diverse group of young women gathered there to work hard in school and to be confident in their abilities. "They spoke from their hearts. You could just see how they understood each other, how they worked together to inspire the crowd," Vicki said.

Meanwhile, in the Oval Office, I looked on as Justin and Barack chatted for about an hour in front of the marble fireplace, with their key advisors gathered around them. There was the presidential seal on the ceiling; there were the portraits of George Washington and Abraham Lincoln; there was the carpet threaded with President Theodore Roosevelt's words: "The welfare of each of us is dependent fundamentally on the welfare of all of us."

In front of me were two men, two world leaders, who understood Roosevelt's words innately, who were joining forces to build a better world, who were embracing diversity and tackling climate change. The mood was electric.

As I listened, I leaned on the president's desk—the Resolute desk, as it's called—and I thought about its Canadian connection. It is made from oak timbers rescued from HMS *Resolute*, a British Royal Navy ship sent to Hudson's Bay in search of the lost Franklin Expedition of 1852. The *Resolute* became locked in ice and then abandoned in 1854, to be salvaged later by the U.S. government and returned to Queen Victoria as a goodwill gesture. Some of its timber was used to build the Resolute desk, which was sent as a gift to Queen Victoria. The Queen gave it back to America in 1880. The wood from that desk had been in Canada and was a chapter in its history. And almost every U.S. president since has used that desk.

In diplomacy and politics, relationships are everything. They take time, energy, and dedication to build. Behind the scenes, my staff and I had worked so hard to develop productive and trusting relationships,

First Lady Michelle Obama and Sophie Grégoire Trudeau at the Let Girls Learn
event.

and in the Oval Office that day, I felt so fortunate to see our plans coming to fruition. I couldn't help but smile as Justin extended his offer to host Barack's visit to Parliament, and with a nod and a few words of thanks, the president accepted. The relationship we had fostered would continue into the future.

After the meeting, we held a press conference in the Rose Garden. The president made remarks to the crowd, welcoming Prime Minister Trudeau and making lighthearted jests.

"There are some things we will probably never agree on," Obama said. "Whose beer is better, who is better at hockey. Where is the Stanley Cup right now? Is it in my hometown with the Chicago Blackhawks?"

When it was Trudeau's turn to speak, he thanked Obama and underscored America's need for strong Canadian exports. "We know for certainty there is a high demand for Canadian goods down here. A few that come to mind that President Obama rightly recognized as being extraordinary contributors to the American success story: Jonathan Toews, Duncan Keith, and Patrick Sharp of the Chicago Blackhawks."

Needless to say, a round of cheers could be heard from all the Canadians in attendance.

Later that day, the State Department and Secretary of State John Kerry hosted a luncheon for all of the American and Canadian guests. As we entered the luncheon, the Stanley Cup was front and center for all to admire. Rufus Wainwright, the American-Canadian singer-songwriter, sang a moving rendition of Canadian Leonard Cohen's "Hallelujah," a song that had been sung at Justin and Sophie's wedding. The couple was so moved that they rushed forward to thank and hug the singer when his song came to an end.

Vicki and I watched all of this happen: the connections being forged, the friendship being honored, and our new friends—these proud Canadians whom we believed in—taking their rightful place on the world stage. *Vogue, Vanity Fair,* and *The New York Times* all ran front-page pieces on the Canadian prime minister, while CBS-TV's *60 Minutes* featured him as well. The media were taken with Trudeau's youth, vigor, and striking good looks, and the stiffness that had marked relations between some American presidents and some Canadian prime ministers had clearly given way to something new and so promising.

I remember everything about those wonderful three days. One of the many highlights was being on the Truman Balcony before the state dinner. The Trudeau family and the Obama family were present. Vicki and Sophie were side by side, enjoying this moment they had helped to create. President Obama talked about the generational aspects of leadership. The past, present, and future coalesced.

But for me, the ultimate highlight was the state dinner in the East Room of the White House, where two hundred guests dined on a meal that combined the best culinary traditions of the United States and Canada. Blooming orchids, hydrangeas, and amaranth in shades of green and white decorated the room to evoke the coming of spring and as a tip of the American hat to Sophie, whose favorite color is green. The live music featured happened to be one of my favorite singer-songwriters, the incomparable Sara Bareilles, from Eureka, California, whom Michelle Obama had invited.

Margaret Trudeau approached me that evening.

"Finally, we meet!" she said. "The kids keep talking about this Bruce guy, and here you are!" She meant her grandchildren, whom we'd met various times in Ottawa.

"Here I am!" I said. "And it is nice to meet you at last. We've heard so much about you." I introduced her to Vicki, and we all talked about how grateful and excited we were to be sharing such a moment.

I have been to many black-tie dinners, but I had not seen anything like this: it was a family meal and a sheer lovefest between our two countries. Others felt it. One senior White House staffer told me later that this dinner was the best she had ever attended during her long years in service.

In his remarks, President Obama reminded guests that we were not at a *dinner*, as Americans say, but a *supper*, as Canadians say. He made jokes about poutine and two-fours of beer—and quipped that he might end the evening with a double-double. The prime minister, for his part, expressed the hope that his hair would turn gray at a slower rate than the president's had.

It was so clear that underlining this humor was a genuine bond between these two men. Trudeau said as much when he remarked that Canadians and Americans are siblings from the same stock. "We are guided by the same core values: respect and co-operation."

Those three days and that dinner set the foundation for the rest of the year. It marked a merging of our two families. We had our old family, the Obamas—with a closeness earned over nearly a decade of working together—and we had our new family, the Trudeaus, who had embraced Vicki and me into their fold. But beyond that, we saw our teams coming together in important ways. All the various departments of the U.S. administration met their Canadian counterparts face-to-face and got a feel for what they could accomplish together after the celebrations. We agreed upon the priorities, and we saw that we could get them done. Would this require negotiation and further diplomacy? Yes, of course. Not all moments in life are pure celebrations. But we knew that if there were disagreements in the future, we could disagree without becoming disagreeable. That's the magic of evolved, mature relationships: there's energy and will to get through the tough stuff.

We were entering a time I think of as a Camelot moment: eighteen months during which two leaders were actually learning from each other, and two countries were learning from each other, too. I did not know then just how much I would come to value that era, one in which maple trees could be planted in Washington as a gift for future generations. I did not know then that the next president of my country would compromise the unity we had strived so long and hard to achieve. Unfortunately, that president would divide the world into us and them,

President Obama at the podium during the state dinner, where he made jokes about poutine, two-fours, and double-doubles.

would bring back the talk of fences and barriers and walls. His defini-
tion of diplomacy would be tit for tat, transactions for the betterment
of "us" at the expense of "them." He would dismantle what should be at
the core of diplomacy—*tikkun olam*—a shared vision of a better world
for all.

Chapter 11

The World Needs
More Canada

Vicki

It was 2016, our last year in Ottawa. We had met so many people; we had worked hard to bring teams together, to make a difference for our country and for Canada. My vision for our community hive was coming together in all kinds of exciting ways. The state dinner was the honey, and there was more honey yet to come—some of it literal.

When Ted Norris and I lifted the frames of our Lornado hive that fall, it was not only buzzing with life but also dripping with rich, golden honey.

"Wow! This is unbelievable!" I said.

"This is one healthy hive," Ted replied.

We harvested a staggering two hundred pounds of honey that year, thanks to the bees of Lornado. We extracted it and put it into two hundred little jars, each one labeled "The Beehives of Lornado Honey, Gift of U.S. Embassy, Ottawa," and decorated with a bright red ribbon.

Our first harvest of honey from the Lornado beehive.

We gave away our bounty to the many guests who passed through the residence, knowing that whatever we shared would come back to us twofold.

But Bruce and I knew we had only a bit of time left in Canada. Our stay was coming to its natural end, and like our Lornado bees, we had ventured out but would soon be returning home. But not then. Not yet.

After the state dinner in 2016, Sophie and I remained as friendly as ever. We would meet for lunch at a little spot in Ottawa called Fraser Café.

One day, we had plans to have lunch at our usual spot. Before our arranged time, Sophie called me.

"It's a lovely day," she said. "I'm coming to pick you up on my Vespa."

"On your Vespa?"

"Yes, why not?"

"Okay," I said with perhaps a little trepidation. "Do you have an extra helmet?"

She did. So we had a date.

The usual protocol when expecting a visitor at Lornado was to let the staff know. But I didn't tell anyone in the residence that day, and I didn't tell the guards at the front gate, either. This was going to be a very fun surprise.

At the agreed-upon time, Sophie arrived at the gate, and soon after, the house staff sought me out to let me know. "Madame Grégoire Trudeau is at the gate, madame."

"Wonderful," I said. "We have lunch plans."

Some *ahem*s and throat clearing. "Madame, she's waiting for you on her Vespa."

"Oh, yes," I replied. "So she is. I'll be her backseat driver."

Without further ado, I went out the front door as Roger and the house staff stared wide-eyed behind me.

I greeted Sophie and then turned back to the speechless staff and said, "Okay, see you later!"

Sophie passed me my helmet. I put it on. And off we went.

Sometimes in life, you just have to live a little.

Thanks to our helmets, nobody recognized us that day as we rode around Ottawa on her motor scooter. But I suspect that back at Lornado, we were much discussed. I imagined the staff speaking in hushed tones about our audacity.

"On a Vespa?" one shocked staff member might have said.

"Yes, on a Vespa!" the other might reply. "I saw it with my own two eyes."

Some head shaking, some tsk-tsks, and some wide smiles.

"Oh, the two madames."

Bruce and his team at the embassy were working hard organizing Obama's upcoming visit. The Liberal Party government was keen to have a state dinner to reciprocate for the amazing time the prime minister had enjoyed in Washington in March. Unfortunately, the president's schedule wouldn't allow for a dinner, but the Canadian team was reluctant to accept a no. That being said, President Obama was indeed coming to Canada. He would arrive in June for the annual North American Leaders Summit, nicknamed the "Three Amigos Summit" because it was bringing together Obama, Trudeau, and the president of Mexico, Enrique Peña Nieto—three leaders with a track record of working well with one another for the mutual benefit of their three countries. Looking back on this now, I can't help but think how incredible it is that just a few years ago, North American leaders could and did regularly negotiate with one another diplomatically and fairly. Now, in the era of Trump, divisiveness abounds, and antagonism rather than unity is the president's modus operandi, much to the detriment of the entire continent.

But in 2016 it was possible to be amigos and behave in a manner befitting leaders. The three heads of state were to discuss a shared commitment to LGBTQ rights (especially poignant in light of the June 12 attack on a gay nightclub in Orlando, Florida, which left forty-nine innocent people dead), renewable energy, and free trade.

For Canadians from coast to coast to coast, the summit was important, but the pinnacle event was Obama speaking at Parliament. To say that Trudeau and his government were excited is an understatement.

When the big day arrived, June 29, 2016, Bruce and I met the president on the tarmac at the Ottawa airport. It was a gorgeous summer day, and the air was electric with our excitement. Governor General David Johnston was with us, along with Canadian Ambassador to the U.S. David MacNaughton, Mayor Jim Watson, and Foreign Affairs Minister Stéphane Dion.

We all knew this was a historic moment. We also knew that Obama's approval rating in Canada was off the charts, which meant he was about to feel the full force of Canadians' adulation. David Johnston could hardly contain himself, but to be fair, none of us could. Bruce and David were good friends by this point; all four of us, including his wife, Sharon, and myself, were close.

As we waited, David turned to Bruce and asked, "So what are you going to say to Obama when he gets off the plane?"

"Well," Bruce said, "I think I'll welcome him to Canada and tell him he's just entered a country where his approval rating is higher than eighty percent. Why do you ask?"

David didn't answer. He just smiled and nodded. He was clearly up to something.

A while later, the plane arrived as scheduled, and before long, the president was walking down the steps to be greeted by all of us.

The first person to welcome him was David.

"Mr. President, it's such an honor to have you visit," he said. "And before Bruce tells you that you have an eighty percent public approval rating in Canada, I want to inform you that Bruce is wrong. You're so loved here that it's actually more like ninety percent. Welcome to Canada!"

Obama shook David's hand and thanked him for the warm welcome. He then moved on to Bruce, who had just been subtly pranked by his friend.

Bruce recovered rather well, though. "Good to see you, sir," he said, and gave Obama his usual big hug.

"Bruce, always a pleasure," the president replied.

Next it was my turn. "It is so wonderful to have you here," I said. "And it's one hundred percent true that Canadians love you."

"Vicki, I'm really happy to be here," he replied. "Michelle sends her best."

From there, the president was whisked away in his limo, nicknamed "the Beast." He attended the North American Leaders Summit with Trudeau and Peña Nieto. He then met with Bruce and other senior advisors for a bilateral meeting. At long last, in the afternoon, it was time for the main event: his speech at Parliament.

I felt so fortunate to be there that day. The room was positively buzzing. Parliament was a hive of activity. Every seat was filled, from the floor to the balcony. The Liberals were on the left, the Conservatives were on the right. Members of the Opposition were hugging members of the Liberal government. The two solitudes crossed party lines to pose together in pictures.

Sophie and Justin walked in with Obama, and we all spontaneously rose to our feet to give him a standing ovation, the first of several he would receive that day. After Trudeau warmly welcomed and introduced him, the president walked to the podium, taking time on the way to shake hands with dignitaries. He tried to quiet the crowd so that he could begin, but there was no way. We were paying our respects. Obama surveyed the room, making eye contact with the crowd, all smiles. And he wasn't alone in that. Everyone was smiling—even the members of the Conservative opposition.

I was a few rows away from the dais in the center of the Parliament floor, and Bruce, having completed his meeting with the president and prime minister, joined me. From our seats, we had a clear view of Sophie and Justin, both of them looking so jubilant, so brimming with excitement and genuine affection for the leader we were about to hear.

President Obama at the North American Leaders Summit with Prime Minister Trudeau and President Enrique Peña Nieto of Mexico. The summit was affectionately called the "Three Amigos Summit."

The room was electric as President Obama entered Parliament to deliver his historic speech.

The energy was palpable; the joy was contagious. I was so proud of the president we represented, and though he was not my prime minister, I was equally proud of Trudeau.

Obama finally managed to quiet the crowd, and we all took our seats. He began to speak, and the room fell to a hush. He thanked Canadians, as well as Justin and Sophie, for making this trip possible. He then reminded everyone that Canada was the very first country he'd visited as president in 2009. "On that visit, I strolled around the ByWard Market, tried a BeaverTail—which is better than it sounds. And I was struck then, as I am again today, by the warmth of the Canadians. . . . We Americans can never say it enough. We could not ask for a better friend or ally than Canada."

He covered many topics during his speech, which lasted nearly an hour. He was often interrupted by peals of applause and laughter. He lauded Canada for championing human rights. He praised its commitment to a set of values whereby all people can make lives for themselves, no matter where they are from, or what their last names are, or what faith they practice.

At certain points, Obama's tone changed, and he warned against those who don't work from a set of values based on justice and equality but from an entirely different set of beliefs. Looking back now, it's as though he were reading America's not-so-distant future.

"Politicians," he said, "some sincere and some entirely cynical, will tap that anger and fear, hearkening back to bygone days of order and predictability and national glory, arguing that we must rebuild walls and disengage from a chaotic world, or rid ourselves of the supposed ills brought on by immigrants, all in order to regain control of our lives."

I couldn't help but think back to my great-grandparents who sought refuge in Canada. What if those unwelcoming walls and impenetrable borders had existed then? What would have happened to them? And would I even have been here now enjoying this incredible moment? I'm certain that many listening to Obama that day—and especially the thousands of Canadians watching from the comfort of their living rooms—had similar thoughts.

The president went on to talk about the everlasting alliance between our two countries and expressed his faith in Trudeau. "My time in office may be nearing an end, but I know that Canada—and the world—will benefit from your leadership for years to come."

When he said, "The world needs more Canada," the crowd erupted in cheers. "Four more years! Four more years!" was chanted over and over again. If only it were possible!

Obama's words were such a compliment to our best friends to the north, and both Bruce and I could not have agreed more that it was entirely earned. And not just 80 percent or 90 percent earned, but the full 100 percent.

Once the speech was over, it was time for a more intimate event, one that both Bruce and I were looking forward to. He had arranged for the president to meet with the embassy staff and their families at the Sir John A. Macdonald Building across the street from Parliament.

We both knew how hard the staff worked. They served their country, and they did so quietly, without a need for praise or fanfare. We wanted to acknowledge them. We wanted them to hear—from the man at the top—that their contributions mattered. That day, the president thanked them personally for their service. He also took the time to pose for photos with their children and families. Those snapshots say it all: beaming staff members proud of their president and proud to be recognized.

After the meet and greet with staff, Bruce and I went to our car and joined the motorcade that would accompany Obama to the airport to bid him farewell. I was seated and buckled in, but before Bruce climbed in, a member of the president's staff flagged him down.

"Mr. Ambassador," he said. "You are requested in the car with the president."

Bruce turned to look at me.

"You heard him. Go!" I said.

Bruce walked up alongside the line of cars and got inside the Beast, the first car in the motorcade.

Apparently, as soon as he was seated, Obama asked, "Where's Vicki?"

"She's four or five cars behind," Bruce said.

"Well, go get her!"

And that's when I heard, "Madame Heyman! Madame Heyman!" being called out by the RCMP, who came to my car door, helped me out, and then escorted me over to the Beast.

The president always sits on the rear passenger-door side. Bruce was seated across from him, and Susan Rice, the president's national security advisor, was next to Bruce.

"Vicki! Did you really think we'd leave without you? Come sit next to me."

So I did.

By this point, Bruce had been through quite a day of summits and discussions and consultations and negotiations. When the president asked him how things were going, he defaulted to a rapid-fire litany of bilateral discussion points and a list of to-dos he hoped to accomplish before the end of his term as ambassador.

The president interrupted him. "No, no, no. I don't mean that. That's all good, but how's it going for you and Vicki personally? You're doing great things in Canada. So what's the real news?"

I jumped in. "Well, we do have some great news, actually. Our daughter Liza, she's getting married. And it's all going to happen on the grounds of Lornado in just a few weeks." Liza had worked in the White House Office of Public Engagement and also at the Department of Homeland Security, so Obama knew her.

"Bruce," the president chided. "You hear that? That's what I'm talking about. *That's* good news."

We spent the rest of our trip to the Ottawa airport catching up on all kinds of things. Bruce soon recovered from his overzealous work mode and joined in with ordinary conversation. We reminisced about the president's first trip to Canada, when he made an unplanned pit stop at the ByWard Market to do some souvenir and sweets shopping. That day, he picked up maple leaf shortbread cookies (now called the "Obama cookie"), a moose key chain, and that BeaverTail pastry.

I can totally understand the president's need for spontaneity every once in a while. Because sometimes you just have to live a little.

At the Ottawa airport, where Air Force One was waiting to take the president home, we said our heartfelt good-byes and bid him adieu.

Afterward, Bruce and I, along with a delegation from Canada 2020, headed over to a bar for a much-needed celebratory drink.

"Thanks, honey," he said.

"For what?" I asked.

"For being the best backseat driver I know."

Just then, Justin Trudeau walked through the doors, a giant smile on his face. He headed straight our way.

"You did it! You brought Obama to Canada!" I said, and gave him a huge hug.

"*We* brought him," he answered. He turned to Bruce. "Bruce, what an incredible day. How are you doing?"

"I'm doing great," he said. "We all need more Canada, but right about now, I think we all need a drink."

Prime Minister Trudeau giving Vicki a hug to celebrate a very successful state visit.

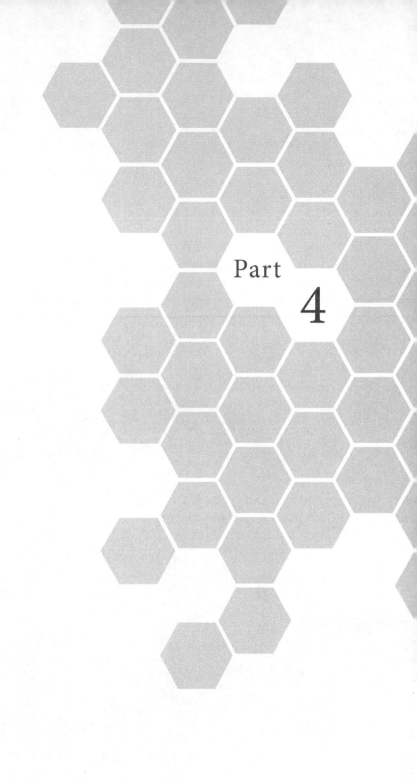

Part

4

Chapter 12

Hindsight

Bruce

As we neared the end of 2016 and the end of our time in Ottawa, one theme recurred not only in our personal story but also in the story of America. That theme can be summarized in a word: hindsight. There was so much we did not know going into that fall season. We did not know that our country was as deeply divided politically and socially as it was. We did not know that the U.S. election, which was right around the corner, would reverse years of stable progress in support of equality and social justice in the United States. We did not know that U.S. policy on refugees and immigration would go from tolerant to xenophobic. We did not know that Donald Trump was about to test our relationship with our greatest ally and friend by attacking long-standing, mutually beneficial trade agreements and undermining the core values that define Canada and Canadians. There was so much we did not see coming. If only we'd known in advance. But it doesn't work that way.

We weren't the only ones feeling blindsided that fall, even before November 8, the day we and our fellow American citizens took to the polls to choose our post-Obama leader. A few weeks prior, I'd flown to Dallas for a meeting between senior officials on the importance of NAFTA. Canadian, American, and Mexican delegates gathered to talk about the importance of the North American relationship, both in terms of trade and the broader relationship that had developed over many years. The meeting had been organized by former president George W. Bush. Though Stephen Harper was no longer prime minister, he attended. I ran into him at the cocktail reception. It was my first time seeing him since the Canadian election a year before. He'd left 24 Sussex Drive with very little fanfare and even fewer farewells. One journalist noted that it was as if he'd left town overnight.

"Stephen," I said. "It's great to see you. How are things going?"

"They're fine, Bruce," he said. "Just fine. How are you? How's Vicki?"

"We're great!" I replied. "Couldn't be better."

There was a pause in our conversation. I considered everything I had learned since taking on the role of ambassador. Those first few months were not easy, and it occurred to me that perhaps my chilly relationship with Harper might have been different had I known just a little bit more about—well, everything. But that's not the way life works. Experience equals time plus challenges faced and overcome.

Before I could think too hard about things, I found myself speaking my thoughts out loud. "I wish I knew when I started this job what I know now," I said.

Stephen paused, took in my comment. Then he nodded.

"You know," he said, "I wish that when I started as prime minister, I knew everything I know now."

I smiled.

So did he.

This was the first personal and meaningful exchange we'd ever had. And I was grateful for it.

Hindsight.

When I returned home from Dallas, much of my attention was on the upcoming American election. As ambassador, it was my duty, required by law, to remain publicly unbiased as to preferences for any party or candidate. It was a bittersweet time, given that Obama, the man Vicki and I had stood behind for years, was stepping down for good. At Lornado, she and I watched pre-election coverage on TV every night. I remember us privately asking each other how it was possible that a reality-TV star with no political experience, dubious claims to success, and who had made overtly racist and sexist remarks could actually be running for the highest office in the land. Was this a practical joke? Was this a serious threat? How had it come to this? It couldn't possibly get worse, right? We are eternal optimists. Little did we know.

It felt a bit odd being away from the United States for the lead-up to the election, and odder still not to be working hard for our candidate Obama. We watched American coverage, but we watched Canadian analysis, too, which seemed to reflect back to us much of our own disbelief and concern about Trump as a candidate. Not being in the States, we didn't really have a grassroots sense of what was happening on the ground. For the first time in years, we weren't directly involved in campaigning, and for the first time ever, we were living away from home.

Meanwhile, on the professional side, Vicki and I still had work to do with regard to the election. We worked hard promoting voter participation by Americans living in Canada. We posted on social media; we talked about the registration processes in our public media conversations; we sent out pamphlets; we took pictures of ourselves filling out our mail-in ballots. The message I repeated over and over to the media was this: "Regardless of who wins, the U.S.-Canada relationship will always be very important." I maintained what I truly believed, that no matter the outcome, the relationship between our two countries would rise above political affiliations, and all would be well. In my heart of hearts, I never imagined that Donald Trump was going to win. And it was beyond my worst imaginings that, as president, he would pose a threat to the sacred bond between our two countries.

The night of the election, Vicki and I hosted a U.S. embassy election party at the Château Laurier hotel ballroom in Ottawa, where our guests could watch the results unfold. We invited media, people from the local business and arts communities, and political people from various levels of Canadian government. Journalists that evening reported live, and TV cameras representing all the major networks were set up at the back of the venue. There was food and music, election trivia, and jumbo screens. There were flags and posters and balloons. There was a general air of anticipation and excitement in the packed room. Across Canada, U.S. consulates were hosting similar events.

Like so many people that day, we went into the event with the expectation that, despite the challenges Hillary Clinton faced in winning over voters—not the least of which was that she was a woman—she would ultimately be declared the victor. After all, here was a candidate with lots of government experience and a proven track record of achieving results. It would be a historic moment for all Americans, and we were ready to celebrate. First, Obama had broken the color barrier when he was elected in 2008, and now, succeeding him, Hillary would shatter the glass ceiling. We would have our first female president.

Everything was going well with our soirée, and the mood in the room was festive. The pundits were making their predictions. Vicki and I walked the floor and greeted our many guests.

But as the night continued, my anxiety began picking up. I'd watched election night events my entire life, and something wasn't right. In fact, something felt very wrong.

"Vicki," I said, "I'm getting a bad feeling about this. What about you?"

If there's one thing I've learned as a husband, it's to trust my wife's instincts. I wasn't asking this lightly. I was asking what her gut was telling her.

"Bruce," she said, "I have a bad feeling, too, but let's stay positive. We've got a long night ahead of us."

Vicki and I had learned a lot from our participation in the Obama campaign. One of the things we recognized were the critical steps in the pathway to victory. The states that Clinton needed most, and the ones that were most telling, were the swing states of Florida, Colorado, Pennsylvania, and Ohio. It was still possible that she could win Ohio and Colorado, lose Pennsylvania and Florida, and still triumph overall. But when Ohio went red, that was not good. And when, a few minutes later, Florida did, too, tensions in our party room began mounting. Pennsylvania was still up for grabs, as were Minnesota and Michigan. There was still a remote hope that things could swing Clinton's way, but the pathways were narrowing. Was there a way to victory? And if not, what would that mean for our country?

By nine o'clock, things were going very poorly. The many guests we'd gathered were getting increasingly nervous. They clearly believed, as we did, that Hillary would emerge triumphant, but when the chances of that became more remote, shock and dismay started to set in. There was nail biting and a lot of edginess. So much for our happy party. The streamers and balloons seemed out of place.

The embassy public affairs team, the media team, the front office team, myself—we all looked like jackrabbits running back and forth, speaking to each other in low tones, contemplating our next steps. The media were watching our every move, too.

Vicki made a call to speak with a good friend of ours who was part of the Clinton camp and who had worked on the campaign alongside her husband. The couple were in Manhattan at the Jacob K. Javits Convention Center, where Clinton and her supporters had gathered to await the election results.

"We can't take it anymore," she told Vicki. "We're leaving."

This was not a good sign.

Around the same time, I received a call from our daughter Liza.

Because she had worked at the Democratic National Committee and the White House, she had friends in Washington, many of whom were deeply embedded in the Clinton campaign.

"Dad," she said, "it's not looking good."

"What do you mean, exactly?" I asked. I was standing in the middle of the party, with cameras all around me. I could see myself projected on the jumbo screens at the back of the room. There I was, looking shocked and dazed with a phone in my hand. The end results had not been called yet.

"Dad?" she said again. "I'm telling you that it's not official yet, but it sure looks like it's over. I think Trump has won."

I was dumbfounded.

I ended the call, and soon after, Vicki appeared by my side.

"Bruce," she said, "you have to do something. No winner has been declared yet. Everyone here is tense. People don't want to be here anymore. Most have already left because they can't bear to watch the results. The rest are just waiting for a statement from you so they can get out of here and watch at home."

"Okay," I said. "Okay."

The room looked barren and desolate. There were only a few stragglers left, but all the reporters remained, though they looked haggard and exhausted and confused. I gathered with the remaining embassy team and quickly prepared to make a statement. In front of the cameras, I said something to this effect: "Thank you so much for coming. It looks like this is going to be a late night, and we may not hear a decision for some time yet . . . and so, thank you for coming. It was a lovely evening, and we'll see where this goes. That's it. Good night."

The election night party we had envisioned had gone completely sideways. On the TV, the talking heads were starting to declare Donald Trump the next president of the United States.

Standing in front of the cameras, making a brief remark at our U.S. embassy election night party in 2016.

"Let's get out of here. Now," Vicki said.

And we did.

We watched the rest of the coverage in the privacy of Lornado, feeling shaken and drained. Like so many other citizens, we just couldn't get our heads around what had happened. We were not in the United States, but we were in a united state of shock. We were also sad, but still, many people—us included—had hope that things would turn out okay; that there would be some continuity in the direction our country was heading under the new president. We had no idea then what was coming.

We were also starting to wonder about my posting as ambassador. What would happen now? Customarily, appointed ambassadors are asked to tender their resignations upon the inauguration of a new president, but there are cases when the new administration requests that an ambassador stay in place during the transition period. When Obama won in 2008, George W. Bush followed protocol and asked his ambassadors to resign, which they did. Obama then asked certain ambassadors to remain at their posts so that there could be a smooth and carefully orchestrated transition between specified outgoing ambassadors and the incoming ones. This way, key negotiations could be contextualized for the new ambassador, and continuity could be preserved—handing the baton, passing the torch.

In the weeks following the election, I received an email from President Obama's chief of staff asking for my letter of resignation effective no later than January 20, 2017, the day of the forty-fifth president's inauguration. It was made clear that if I wanted to leave earlier, I could. But I had not heard anything from the Trump administration about next steps, so I felt a bit in limbo. Surely they would reach out and state their preferences? Surely they would opt for the torch to be passed rather than dropped at such a key moment of transition? Surely the flame would burn on?

"We should leave on January 20," Vicki said. "It's time."

I wasn't so sure. At any point, the Trump team could ask me to stay.

Was it not the right thing to do—my duty, in fact—to oblige in that case?

"Bruce," Vicki said on the many nights when we discussed this, "you took on your role as President Obama's personal representative. If you stay on, you'd be Trump's personal representative. Have you seriously considered that? Have you considered what that really means?"

Of course I had. But I was conflicted. I'd sworn to preserve and protect the U.S. Constitution and to serve my country. If I were truly non-partisan, that meant serving my country no matter who was in power—at least for a while. In such a role, I could offer important information about the current state of negotiations and communications between the United States and Canada. Wouldn't that be best for America? But no matter how many times I put this argument to Vicki, she didn't agree.

"I don't want to stay here to serve the new administration," she said, which, of course, gave me pause.

On December 7, after making several attempts to contact the new administration, I still had heard nothing. I decided to write the Trump transition team a very short letter in which I explained my familiarity with matters as diverse as national security and commerce. I said I was open to discussing transition possibilities, though I certainly didn't commit myself to anything.

The day after I sent my letter, outgoing Vice President Joe Biden was in Ottawa. When we couldn't make the Obama dinner happen, we worked with the Canadian government to bring in Biden for a state dinner. There were very few people that Vicki and I felt we could consult for advice on what to do vis-à-vis the silence from the new administration. We needed help from someone who could understand all sides.

"Joe Biden will know what's best," Vicki said.

"You're right. Let's ask him."

We met Biden at the Ottawa airport and drove with him to the state dinner.

"If we're given the opportunity to stay on, should we?" I asked him.

"You're not going to like my answer, Bruce," he said. "First, I doubt you'll be given the opportunity to stay. But if I'm wrong, and you are, then, yes, you should stay."

I looked at Vicki's serious expression. She was listening intently to what was being said—and to what wasn't.

"Look," said Joe, "we need people like you and Vicki representing our country during this time."

Vicki nodded.

"Thanks, Joe," I said. After that conversation, Vicki and I agreed that if given the opportunity, we would continue to serve our country. But Biden turned out to be right.

Days and weeks drifted by with no contact from Trump's team. And the response to my letter?

Crickets.

Finally, it was nearing the winter holidays. Vicki and I went to Colorado to ring in the New Year with our family. After that, we were invited to the White House along with many other ambassadors and their spouses. While there, Obama thanked us for our service. He was still optimistic about the future of America and urged us to be, too. He said that perhaps our country may take a few steps back, but he had faith in the next generation, which he saw as strong and forward thinking. Vicki and I took solace in those words. Right to his last days in power, Obama was giving others hope and the resilience to carry on.

Vicki and I returned to Ottawa on January 3, 2017. There were still no clear answers. But on January 5, *The New York Times* published an article with the headline "In Break with Precedent, Obama Envoys Are Denied Extensions Past Inauguration Day." It became clear that all of Obama's ambassadors were to go. But what was also abundantly clear is that the Trump transition team hadn't told any of us directly. How did we hear about this decision? Through an article in *The New York Times*.

Back at Lornado, the staff were very gracious and kind but also very clear about what needed to happen. They'd been to this rodeo before.

"Madame, sir, we realize there's no response from the new administration, but we feel that, too, is a response. We are so sad to see you go. We will do everything we can to make this as easy as possible. There's a lot of packing to do, and we're going to begin that now."

"Of course," Vicki said. "And thank you. We couldn't ask for a better staff than all of you. You really are incredible."

She then made one request. "Is it okay," she asked, "if the art goes last?"

"Of course, madame. We understand. There will be art until the end."

The art, for us, was the life of Lornado, and for our few remaining days, we needed that comfort. We did not want to be looking at blank walls. We were not alone in feeling disconsolate. We could see it in the faces of the staff, too. The tears brushed from eyes, the slumped shoulders, the hushed tones. Seeing Chuck Close's Obama portrait—the very picture of hope and equality. And Marie Watt's blanket sculpture—the resonant voices of past generations stitching together past, present, and future. And Ed Burtynsky's *Colorado River Delta #2*—a clarion call to action, guiding us to protect our fragile waterways and land. All of the art provided solace and a reminder of the values that we stood for. These artistic creations symbolized for us, now more than ever, what we had to keep fighting for.

I came across Vicki in the library one day with a look of contemplation on her face as she surveyed the room. The art was still there, but much of the furniture had been cleared out.

"Honey, what's up? Are you worried?" I asked.

"Not about me," she said. "I'm worried about where the United States is headed."

She was putting into words a sentiment that was pulsing through the entire residence and the embassy. It was a sentiment we knew was being felt by many of our fellow Americans, too.

On January 8, at long last, I received a call from someone on the Trump transition team in Washington.

She had a very high, squeaky voice. She sounded young—possibly an intern (or an elementary school student).

"Sir, I'm-calling-all-ambassadors-to-see-if-you-have-any-specific-health-issues-that-may-preclude-you-from-leaving-or-any-family-members-or-children-who-may-be-impeding-your-quick-departure," she said so rapidly and so formulaically that it was clear she was reading from a script.

"Uh, no," I said categorically. "My wife and I have no such issues, but actually, I would be happy to provide a substantial briefing to the incoming ambassador. I sent a letter to the incoming administration on December 7 about this very topic. Do you have a response on that?"

A long pause and some papers shuffling. "Um . . . well . . . that sounds really cool. So, like, should I . . . maybe have someone call you back about that?"

It was clear she hadn't the faintest clue how to proceed, so much so that I actually started to feel sorry for her.

"That would be good, yes," I said.

"Okay, so. Yeah."

"And when can I expect to hear back?"

Another long pause. "Um . . . maybe, like, tomorrow morning?"

"That'll do," I said.

I'm sure she was relieved when I said good-bye.

The next day, I received no calls. But I did have the cell phone number of the woman who had called me. I called it several times. There was no answer and no voice mail. I decided to contact a few other U.S. ambassadors. Had they received the same call? Turns out, they had—from the very same woman. They, too, were ringing back her cell number, to no avail.

As it turned out, that was the only phone call I would ever receive from the Trump transition team.

It was the second week of January when the moving trucks were at Lornado's door ready to take many of our possessions back home to

Chicago. All the time we were packing, we were also saying our good-byes. We'd made so many friends in Ottawa, and it was hard to leave them behind. During the day, we did farewell interviews with various media outlets, and in the evenings there were dinners and events.

We invited Sophie, Justin, and the kids for a casual dinner with us at Lornado one last time, along with his chief of staff, Katie Telford and her son. As usual, when we opened the front door, there were big hugs and kisses, but I think we all felt the bittersweet tinge of the moment, too. The children were very excited and rushed off to the kitchen because Chef Dino had kindly offered to teach them how to make salads and bake cookies. This gave the adults some time to adjourn to the library and talk. We chatted about the recent election, of course, and Trudeau was hopeful as always. The prime minister and his team had already met with the Trump team. They had talked about improving NAFTA and trade, and they were optimistic that they could build a relationship with the new president. I think we were all doing our best to be positive and to continue doing what we had always done together: build bridges.

When it was time for dinner, the children came out of the kitchen, proudly carrying their amazing salad creations, which they presented to all the guests with great fanfare. They were wide-eyed and brimming with enthusiasm and joy. They were just what we all needed. I hoped that one day those children would grow up and remember all the good times they had in Ottawa when their father was prime minister, which is exactly what Justin has expressed looking back on his own childhood.

That was a family dinner; a truly great one. We exchanged toasts. I spoke about the professional aspects of our relationship—how it had been such a pleasure to work with Justin and Katie, and his entire team. I also spoke about how the U.S.-Canada relationship would endure any-thing. I said I felt optimistic because I knew the prime minister and his family would continue to lead their country in the right direction. Vicki spoke about what a privilege it was to know both Sophie and Justin, how we were so proud and grateful to call them friends. For their part,

(*From left to right*): Katie Telford's son George, Prime Minister and Sophie Trudeau with their children Ella Grace and Xavier making cookies with Chef Dino at Lornado.

Sophie and Justin expressed their sadness to see us go but added that they knew we would remain close, even if we no longer lived in the same country. It was especially poignant to watch Sophie and Vicki enjoy their remaining time together. Vicki hugged her friend good-bye and slipped Sophie a note she'd written: "Strong women: may we know them, may we be them, may we raise them."

The entire evening felt like a Thanksgiving dinner. It was far too late to hit the American date and far too early for the Canadian one—but it was a Thanksgiving dinner nonetheless.

On January 17 we had a farewell reception at the embassy. So many people showed up: probably close to three hundred. It was yet another bittersweet occasion. Vicki and I both made remarks. This was a time to speak from the heart. We expressed our gratitude to everyone who had helped us for three years. I talked about the various roles we all had, and how everyone had come together as a community to make things work. I recognized Vicki's role as a cultural envoy—even though she had no official title, that is what she had been. This was met with much applause.

"I want you to know that Vicki and I will never forget our time here, and we will never forget any of you. You're family now, and I hope you all feel that. We came to this country liking Canada, but we are leaving loving Canada."

For her part, Vicki spoke about how life is a journey that takes you to so many unexpected and exciting places. She thanked everyone for making her feel welcome at the embassy and for working with her to create a hive of community activity that she knew would continue on. She was wearing a bracelet—beads on leather—that a friend had brought back from Africa years earlier. The beads spelled out *Obama*. She wore it frequently during Barack's first election campaign, and on the night of our good-bye, she put it on again.

"We have an opportunity," she said. "We are still on our journey, all of us together." She reminded them of President Obama's campaign motto, "Yes we can."

"We can still contribute to the work," she said. "Now more than ever. 'Yes we will' must be our new anthem."

We left that party feeling mixed emotions, but we knew this was not a good-bye. Canada had taught us another life lesson: that *au revoir* is a much better option than *good-bye*.

Afterward, we headed back to Lornado with leftover trays of food. We went straight to the kitchen, where the staff were gathered. We were all exhausted. They had been helping us pack, working their fingers to the bone, organizing all aspects of our two-week good-bye. We cracked open champagne. We opened up the leftover food trays and ate with our hands. We hugged one another. We had learned from our Newfoundland friends how to have an impromptu kitchen party, and that's just what we did. We joked and laughed and teased one another. We reminisced.

"Do you remember the day, madame, when you took off on Madame Trudeau's Vespa?"

"Sir, I'll never forget when you lit a few logs in the fireplace and almost re-created the Ottawa Valley's Great Fire of 1870."

"Remember Theaster and Séan McCann singing 'Amazing Grace'? I almost dropped the tray I was carrying."

These dedicated people had worked with us for three years, and in everything they did, there was care and devotion that went way beyond just "doing the job." Every holiday celebration, every event, every dinner, every detail, every hard knock—they'd been right beside us. There were no secrets. There was so little strife. We were more than a team. We were family.

For three years, Roger had a running joke with Vicki. She would ask him who his favorite ambassador was. He'd get that twinkle in his eye, that little smile at the corners of his mouth. "I don't pick favorites, madame, as I've told you so many times before."

That night, as everyone enjoyed the kitchen party, Vicki sidled up to Roger one last time.

Dancing with Roger at our farewell
party on our last night in Lornado.

"Roger," she said, "this could be the very last time you get a chance to answer my question. So tell me honestly, of all the ambassador husband-and-wife teams you've served over the last twenty-five years, Bruce and I are your favorite, right?"

"Madame," he replied, "you know that I cannot choose favorites."

"Okay," Vicki persisted. "Maybe Bruce isn't your favorite ambassador, but I'm your favorite madame. Admit it!"

There was that twinkle again. "I will say this. I have learned a lot about the art of diplomacy from you. And if I were to choose a favorite madame, it is possible that I would choose you."

"Oh, Roger!" Vicki said, pulling him in for a hug. "I always knew I was your favorite!"

"Madame, I never said that!" he insisted. But he embraced her nonetheless.

That was a late night, but a great one. The next morning, it was time for us to leave Lornado for good. Even the art was gone from the walls. When it was time for us to depart, our Lornado family gathered at the front door. There are people to whom you are so grateful that there are no words to adequately capture what they mean to you. There are times when words don't need to be spoken. And that morning, our hearts spoke volumes to one another.

Vicki and I got into the car that would take us to the airport. We waved back at our Lornado family, and we drove away from the residence for the last time.

Au revoir, Canada, I thought to myself.

Because I knew this was not good-bye.

Saying good-bye to our wonderful house staff, who made our time in Lornado so special and became our Lornado family.

Chapter 13

The Queen Bee
Leaves the Hive

Vicki

There is a memory of our time in Canada that I turn over in my mind again and again, like a worry stone. It was May 2014, when Bruce and I visited Peggy's Cove in Halifax. That was an incredible trip. It was our first time visiting the cove, and we were amazed and impressed by the stark coastline and the towering lighthouse that guided fishermen back to shore. We wandered around the rocky shoreline and walked the docks where the fishermen were taking in their catches for that day. The sea looked endless. The boats returning to the harbor were colorful and bright. On the shore were nets and ropes heaped in coils and awaiting their next voyage out to sea.

There was a fisherman on his deck. He'd just docked and was taking in his haul. Each of his hands held a stack of glistening, multicolored starfish. Some were dark orange, almost rust colored. Others were earthen brown. Still others were blushing pink and a deep, rich purple.

Starfish, the jewels of the sea, in Peggy's Cove.

The array of colors and sizes took my breath away. They were jewels of the sea. And they were alive. I was spellbound.

"Hi!" I called out. "Did you just catch all of those?"

"Yes, ma'am," he said. "I was out there fishing. Sometimes I like to collect starfish. I've been catching them for years. I bring them up, admire them, then I put them back where they belong. Would you like to see them up close?"

"I sure would," I said.

He gestured for me to hold out my palms, which I did. Then he transferred a pumpkin-orange starfish into my hands. It rippled and flexed. I could feel how strong it was, how it gripped me. I could smell the salt of its ocean home.

"Wow, it's astonishing," I said. "They're all different colors."

"Ah, yes," he replied. "No two alike, as far as I can tell. That's the beauty of the starfish."

"There are so many!"

"Oh, not so, ma'am," he said. "They're disappearing. In the old days, starfish were everywhere. I'd bring them in by the bucketful. But not now."

"Do you know why?" I asked.

The lines in his face seemed to get a little deeper. "'Fraid I don't for sure," he said. "The ocean has changed a lot. Might be that we don't care for it like we once did. Take too much from it, don't give enough back. But as long as there are starfish, I'll always take a moment to appreciate them."

"Yes, I can see why you'd do that," I said.

The fisherman and I stood on the shore for a few minutes, trading starfish back and forth, admiring their color and shape and diversity. He held each one so gently. I felt such an array of emotions: awe and wonder . . . and sadness. Here was this man, this caretaker of the sea, who was so generously sharing with me one of the hidden marvels of his profession and one of his great fears, too: that the ocean's bounty might be running out. There was such reverence in him; such quiet respect for the natural world. But there was sadness there, too. What would the future hold? Had we asked too much of this precious resource, the ocean? And if so, was it too late to make a change? He held those starfish in his hands as a lament and as a prayer: *What have we done, and is it too late to change?*

Recently, I've been returning to that memory with greater frequency. We are not so different from starfish. We are all unique, and we are all the same. We are all awe-inspiring, and we are all as fragile as the planet we call our home. We can thrive and grow and prosper in the right environment. But if we don't care for it, if we take our home for granted, we risk losing the very environment that makes us who and what we are. We also need to listen carefully to what the environment is telling us and to those who know it best.

Canada, for me, had become a new home and a sanctuary. It was a place where I thrived. I tackled new situations, new problems there. So when January 2017 came along, it was hard to leave. That's the beauty of opportunity: seizing it means pushing past your own boundaries to find greater stamina and strength. I left knowing that the country and its people had changed me for the better, and I hoped that in some small way, I'd also left my mark. I knew that I'd continue to work with many of the Canadian partners in my hive and that the treasured friendships Bruce and I had made would endure and prosper long after we left Ottawa. As I sat in the airport waiting to go back home, I knew my work would continue; that I would still be a cultural leader, an advocate of the arts, and a bridge builder between the United States and Canada. The friendships Bruce and I had made were permanent; they were cemented. Whether chosen or forged through the bond of blood, family is family.

Bruce and I needed stamina more than ever when we returned home to the United States. It was a different country from the one we'd left just a few years before. We were in disbelief as we watched Donald Trump's inauguration. We reflected on the Obama decade and all that he had accomplished in the United States: Obamacare, a renewed and prosperous economy, environmental protections, increasing social justice for diverse communities. The United States had garnered the respect and admiration of the world during Obama's tenure. Our country extended friendship and support to our allies in global health, trade, and defense. In return, we received the trust of many foreign nations that worked with us co-operatively and collaboratively. Obama's leadership brought us to a zenith on the world stage. Multilateralism was our road map. We felt so much enduring pride in these national accomplishments and hoped that the new administration would embrace the best of this legacy. But those hopes were dashed almost immediately. We were saddened to see that there was no interest from the new administration to leverage or continue on the path we had forged. We were left with the sinking feeling that the social, cultural, and political values we'd worked to cultivate were endangered.

I kept reminding myself that although Trump was the president, he did not represent all Americans. Only 57 percent of eligible U.S. voters had cast ballots. Donald Trump captured 47 percent of those votes. That meant his leadership was bestowed upon him by 27 percent of the voting American population. So what about the other 73 percent of Americans who voted for someone else or didn't vote at all?

A few days after we returned to the States, we attended the Sundance Film Festival in Park City, Utah. Bruce and I had financially supported several films that were premiering in the festival: films about social justice, youth empowerment, global health, and the protection of endangered species. Going to Sundance gave us a sense of hope that no matter who resided in the White House, we the people would continue to advocate for the things that mattered to us most and connected us as human beings. Showing our passion and concern for these issues filled us up during this unsettling time, as it still does today.

On Saturday, January 21, Bruce and I joined the Women's March in Park City. This historic march was occurring in cities not only across

America but also around the world. Millions demonstrated. It was the first protest march we had ever participated in. We felt compelled to stand up against bigotry and discrimination. It was a cold, snowy day, but we felt a warmth by being there and expressing our views with thousands of people. It felt as though we were uniting with those tens of millions of Americans who were not in favor of Trump and his belief system. People were actively protesting both Trump's inauguration and his misogynist statements. Americans of all ages and backgrounds were standing up for human rights, freedom of religion, and racial and gender equality. We walked side by side with legions of marchers carrying signs that read "There is beauty and strength in diversity," and "Giving rights to others does not take rights from you," and "Real men don't grab it." The outpouring of emotions was palpable. Bruce and I felt a sense of community return to us: our country was torn and divided, but those peaceful protesters were as horrified by the changing political and social landscape as we were. We did not know what the future held, but at least we knew we were not alone.

The future came fast and furiously. On January 27 Trump signed an executive order banning entry into the United States for people from Iraq, Syria, Iran, Libya, Somalia, Sudan, and Yemen—all Muslim-majority countries. The order was especially cruel toward Syrian refugees, coming at a time when so many people from that war-torn country were desperately seeking safe haven not only in Europe but also around the world. Immediately after its signing, planes were turned around midflight, and people on their way to the United States—travelers who would have been permitted entry days earlier—were suddenly turned away solely on the basis of their nationality. Family members in airports across the country waited in vain for loved ones. Was this really happening? Could personal freedoms be crushed so quickly? The answer was yes.

Just as we took solace from American protesters, we also took comfort in Canada's reaction to Trump's orders. On January 28 Prime

On January 21, 2017, Bruce and I joined millions of others at the Women's March. We felt a much-needed sense of community in a country that was divided.

Minister Trudeau made his nation's position clear. I remember the tweet he sent on that day: "To those fleeing persecution, terror, and war, Canadians will welcome you regardless of your faith. Diversity is our strength. #WelcomeToCanada." That hashtag trended on Twitter soon after.

That was the first instance of Canada standing in opposition to the values and foreign policies of the Trump administration. It was not to be the last. As we look north from our U.S. vantage point, we continue to gather comfort and strength from Canada as a champion of equality and justice in an era of great uncertainty.

Seven months earlier, in June 2016, Bruce and I received some great news: the biological diversity and wildlife-friendly grounds and gardens at Lornado were being recognized. The U.S. National Wildlife Federation designated the residence a Certified Wildlife Habitat. We were told that Lornado was the first official foreign U.S. residence to be recognized in this way. Bruce and I, along with the entire staff, were so proud of this accolade. We'd seen first-hand how the gardens teemed with life: from birds, to butterflies, to groundhogs, to foxes. There was even a resident deer who made such frequent appearances that our granddaughters Clara and Emma named her Emily. And, of course, there were the bees, which were so copious and such busy pollinators that we'd had an incredible first-year yield of honey.

When Bruce and I left Lornado, we were confident that even though we wouldn't be there to see it, come spring, the seeds we had sown would flourish. The bees remained on the premises all winter, living in the hives in a dormant state.

But in the spring of 2017, just a few months after we'd left, we learned some troubling news from the Lornado staff: the queen bee was gone. She'd simply up and left when the snow melted, taking her brood with her.

For the foreseeable future, at least, there would be no more bees or honey at Lornado. There would be no hives at all.

The Art of Diplomacy

Bruce

There's an interesting confluence of American and Canadian interaction that happens along the border between Canada and the United States. But nowhere is this more powerful or more profound than at Niagara Falls. There, our two countries come together geographically, geopolitically, and environmentally. We share its water, and we share the power that it generates. More than three thousand tons of water flow over Niagara Falls every second, and it is capable of producing more than four million kilowatts of electricity for Canada and the United States.

There are three falls that make up Niagara—Horseshoe Falls, which straddle the border, and on the U.S. side, the American Falls and Bridal Veil Falls. Every year, millions of tourists come from all corners of the earth to witness its grandeur. The water thunders over that majestic edge heedless of which country it is in. We can say that this piece of the falls is on the American side and that piece is on the Canadian side, but the water rushes where it will. From its starting point in the United States, it travels freely all the way down the Niagara River, then to Lake Ontario, through the Saint Lawrence River, and, finally, out to the vast Atlantic Ocean. Water knows no owners or stakeholders, no ours and theirs, no boundaries or limits, despite the borders human beings assign it. Water reminds us to share and to respect, because the water on my side will be on your side soon enough.

When it comes to land, Barack Obama acknowledged how rare it is that two countries can share a border the way we do, with equanimity and respect. During his Canadian visit in 2016, he said, "In a world where too many borders are a source of conflict, our two countries are joined by the longest border of peace on earth."

When I became ambassador in 2014, there were four quotes from American presidents engraved on the walls leading to the ambassadorial suite of the U.S. embassy in Ottawa. But when Vicki and I left Canada, there were five. We added President Obama's words about our border being the longest border of peace on earth.

Vicki and I honored the president at Lornado as well. We planted a tree in front of the residence, the first of its kind, with a plaque to commemorate his speech at Parliament and his visit to Ottawa. Vicki intentionally had that tree planted right in the front so that all future ambassadors and visitors would pass it every day. The world needs more Canada, and more trees.

I am no longer the U.S. ambassador to Canada, but I'm often called upon to talk about the special relationship between our two countries. In a time when that bond is being challenged more than ever before, we all need reminders that we have something to lose, a precious resource that we must protect, as foundational and life-sustaining as water. It's called friendship.

We are family, no matter what, but the bond between us is fragile. Vicki and I now consider ourselves citizen ambassadors for the Canada-U.S. relationship. We are private citizens working to make a difference.

We continue to pollinate ideas. We find like-minded artists, thought leaders, politicians, businesspeople, and change makers who are invested in *tikkun olam*, and we invite them to our hive. We are, like so many other Americans and Canadians, descendants of immigrants who came to North America in search of better lives for themselves and their children.

Canadians and Americans share a respect for social justice, an entrepreneurial spirit, and a deep sense of loyalty to their families and to the land. Right now the moral compass of North America points north, and as we follow it, Vicki and I feel hopeful about what we see. Barack Obama led with his heart and conscience, and we see Canadian leaders doing that as well, rather than out of anger and threats, force and fear.

If we have learned anything from Canadians, it is that diplomacy is an art. It behooves us to make a point without making an enemy, to break bread rather than agreements, to open doors rather than build

walls, to celebrate differences rather than suppress them, to protect our resources—and each other. Because as John F. Kennedy once said about the relationship between our two countries, "Those whom nature hath so joined together, let no man put asunder. What unites us is far greater than what divides us."

The question is: Can we keep it that way?

The answer is simple: yes we can.

Acknowledgments

Our sincerest thanks to our countries' extraordinary leaders:
President Barack Obama and First Lady Michelle Obama
His Excellency Prime Minister Justin Trudeau and Sophie Grégoire Trudeau
The Honorable Stephen Harper and Laureen Harper
Former Governor General David Johnston and Sharon Johnston
Former Governor General Michaëlle Jean
Mayors Jim Watson, Naheed Nenshi, John Tory, and Denis Coderre

Our publishing team:
Our writing collaborator and editor, Nita Pronovost
Our publisher, Kevin Hanson
Felicia Quon, Catherine Whiteside, Greg Tilney, Sophia Muthuraj, and
    our entire Simon & Schuster Canada team
Our literary agent, Samantha Haywood, Transatlantic Agency President
Anne Tate Pearce, Cary Goldstein, and the Simon & Schuster New York team

Our uncharted team:
Lauren Eiten, Randi Lawrence, Lydia Slaby, Alison Heyman, Liza
    Heyman, Lou Harrison, Eric Katz, Lisa Weaver, and John Spears

Our Lornado family:
Roger Beauregard, Jean-François Traversy, Dino Ovcaric, Andrew
    Sasaki, Lori Duval, Miranda Kelly, Imelda Mejia, and Stella Buanviaje

241

Beekeepers Ted Norris and Donna Davies
Gillian Catrambone
Anna Khimasia

Our children and grandchildren:
David and Alison Heyman, Liza and Brian MacCarthy, Caroline and
   Zak Rudzki, Emma, Clara, and Brooks Heyman

Our parents and siblings:
Sherry and Miles Heyman, Sharon and Robert Simons, Wendy Heyman
   and Armin Sabeti, Richard and Alyse Heyman, Gwen and Brian
   McCallion, Spencer and Debra Simons, and our nieces and nephews

Our treasured friends:
From our beginnings, through our years in Chicago, to our Obama family and our Canadian friends, thank you for being our teachers and a
part of our story. There are too many to name—trust us, we tried—but
each one of you contributed to make our hive buzz. Thank you.

U.S. government partners:
Illinois Senator Richard Durbin
Minnesota Senator Amy Klobuchar
Former Commerce Secretary Penny Pritzker
The U.S. State Department and special thanks to the Canada desk,
   Ambassador Roberta Jacobson, Sue Saarnio, Lauren Bernstein, and
   Jennifer Wicks
The National Security Council
Agencies of the U.S. government that work on the Canada-U.S.
   relationship daily

Canadian government partners:
Global Affairs Canada

National Capital Commission
The Prime Minister's Cabinet
Members of Parliament
The Senate of Canada

U.S. embassy team across Canada, with special thanks to:
Richard Sanders and Elizabeth Aubin
The U.S. Embassy Leadership team
The U.S. Marines
U.S. Consuls General
Sarah Goldfeder
Kundai Mashingaidze
Kay Mayfield, Steve Posivak, and the entire public affairs team
Penny Wieser
Katrina Lauzon
Charlie and Kate Brandeis
Peter Kujawinski
Wendy Williams

Former U.S. ambassadors to Canada and their partners, who showed us the ropes:
Ambassador David Jacobson and Julie Jacobson
Ambassador Gordon Giffin and Patty Giffin
Ambassador Jim Blanchard and Janet Blanchard
Ambassador David Wilkins and Susan Wilkins

Canadian ambassadors to the U.S.:
Ambassador David MacNaughton
Former Ambassador Gary Doer

Royal Canadian Mounted Police (RCMP/GRC):
Who provided protection, direction, and friendship

Canadian and American media:
For working every day to get the story right

Art and culture partners:
Art in Embassies, U.S. Department of State—Camille Benton, Jamie
    Arbolino, Welmoed Laanstra, and Ellen Sussman
American supporters who generously lent us works of art for our
    Contemporary Conversations exhibition at Lornado—Larry and
    Marilyn Fields, Paul and De Gray, Bob Chase and HEXTON Modern
    and Contemporary, Michael and Barbara Gamson, Richard Gray
    Gallery and Alex Katz, Edward Burtynsky, Marie Watt and PDX
    Contemporary Art, Eric Fischl, Stephen and Bette Wilkes
Artists participating in Contemporary Conversations—Marie Watt,
    Nick Cave, Eric Fischl, Stephen Wilkes, Kiki Smith, Theaster Gates,
    and Anne Chu (in memoriam)
National Gallery of Canada—Mark Mayer, Michelle Robitaille, and team
Curators at the National Gallery of Canada—Josée Drouin-Brisebois,
    Jonathan Shaughnessy, Greg Hill, Rhiannon Vogl, and Katerina
    Atanassova
National Arts Centre—Christopher Deacon, Peter Herrndorf, Jayne
    Watson, and Alexander Shelley
Canada Council for the Arts—Simon Brault
Students on Ice—Geoff Green
Ming Tiampo, professor of art history at Carleton University
Zita Cobb, Fogo Island Arts
Tony Hayton, Florida Highwaymen art exhibit
Lornado docents—Cayllan Cassavia and Manon Gaudet

Organizations in our hive:
Aga Khan Museum
American Chamber of Commerce in Canada (AmCham Canada)
Anthropocene Project

Art Gallery of Ontario

Banff Forum

Business Council of Canada

C2 Montréal

Canada 2020

Canadian Canoe Museum

Canada Institute at the Wilson Center (U.S.)

Canadian American Business Council (CABC)

Canadian Chamber of Commerce

Canadian Museum of History

Canadian Museum for Human Rights

Canadian Museum of Nature

Carleton University

Chicago Council on Global Affairs (U.S.)

Chicago Ideas (U.S.)

Chicago Media Project (U.S.)

Council for Canadian American Relations (CCAR)

Council of the Great Lakes Region (CGLR)

DARKSPARK

Economic Club of Chicago (U.S.)

Eli's Cheesecake Company (U.S.)

Embarc Chicago (U.S.)

Equal Voice Facing History and Ourselves (U.S.)

Fogo Island Arts–Shorefast Foundation

Foreign Policy for America (U.S.)

Fulbright Canada

Hnatyshyn Foundation

Hot Docs Canadian International Documentary Festival

iHuman Youth Society

Impact Hub Ottawa

Invest for Kids (U.S.)

Jewish Federation

McGill University

Meridian International Center (U.S.)

Michaëlle Jean Foundation

Montreal Museum of Fine Arts

Nature Conservancy (U.S.)

National Arts Centre

National Gallery of Canada

National Security Action (U.S)

Niagara College

Niagara University (U.S.)

Obama Foundation (U.S)

OCAD University

Ottawa Art Gallery

Partners in Art

Power Plant

Renaissance Society (U.S.)

Rideau Hall Foundation

Royal Ontario Museum (ROM)

Run for Something (U.S.)

SheEO

Students on Ice

Toronto International Film Festival (TIFF)

Trust 15

University of Calgary

University of Ottawa

University of Toronto

Vanderbilt University (U.S.)

Walrus

WE Charity

When We All Vote

Writers' Trust of Canada

Appendix

Heyman Honey Cake

Vicki

It is a Jewish tradition to mark important events (such as Rosh Hasha-nah, the Jewish New Year) and milestones (such as the birth of a child) with honey and sometimes with honey cake. My grandmother made great Jewish food, and her best dish was brisket. She would on occasion make a honey cake, using a recipe from a Jewish community cookbook given to her by my dear great-aunt, Betty Korros, who is an amazing baker.[1] Bruce's family likewise embraced the tradition of honey cake. In a letter from Bruce's great-grandfather in Lithuania to his grandfather Samuel in the United States, the older man thanks his son for sending a honey cake in honor of the birth of his new American granddaughter.

When Bruce and I left Lornado, we took a few jars of our honey with us as a sweet reminder of our time in Canada. I was hoping to use a little bit of that honey to make a celebratory honey cake, but, alas, it was not meant to be. We brought the jars to Aspen, Colorado, where Bruce and I spend a lot of time hiking and skiing. But in the summer of 2017, some six months after we left Ottawa, there was a break-in. A bear had gotten into the pantry. It helped itself to steaks, some wine—and the last jars of Lornado honey.

As our parting gift to you, dear friends, Bruce and I offer you our treasured family recipe for honey cake—complete with metric and imperial measurements to please both Canadian and American bakers.

We thank you for going on this journey with us, and we welcome you to our hive. May you savor and share all the sweetness that life has to offer.

Heyman Honey Cake

For the Cake

¾ cup (180 ml) butter

¾ cup (180 ml) sugar

3 eggs

1 cup (250 ml) all-purpose sifted flour

1½ teaspoons (7.5 ml) baking powder

¼ teaspoon (1 ml) salt

½ teaspoon (2.5 ml) cinnamon

¼ cup (60 ml) milk

½ teaspoon (2.5 ml) grated orange rind

1 cup (250 ml) pecans or walnuts, chopped

For the Syrup

½ cup (125 ml) sugar

1 cup (250 ml) honey

¾ cup (180 ml) water

1 teaspoon (5 ml) lemon juice

Yield: one 8-by-8-inch (20-by-20-cm) cake, about 36 pieces

Preparation time: about 60 minutes

Preheat your oven to 350 F (175 C). Grease and sprinkle flour on an 8-by-8-inch (20-by-20-cm) cake pan. Cream together the sugar and butter. Add the eggs. Sift together the dry ingredients and combine with the wet batter. Add the milk and the orange rind. Beat well. Next, fold in the nuts. Pour the entire mixture into your prepared pan and bake for about 30 minutes, until the middle feels spongy when touched.

While you wait, mix up some syrup: combine honey, sugar, water, and lemon juice in a medium saucepan and simmer for 5 minutes. Skim and cool in the fridge.

Remove your cake from the oven after about 30 minutes. Cut it into pieces while it's hot. Pour the cooled syrup over your pieces. Refrigerate to let the syrupy sweetness soak in.

Notes

Chapter 4: In Bed with an Elephant

1. Canada 2020, "Canada 2020: Ambassador Bruce Heyman Q&A with Frank McKenna (Full)," June 2, 2014, Vimeo, https://vimeo.com/97233500.

Chapter 7: A Healthy Hive

1. Edward Burtynsky, "Water: Artist's Statement," Edward Burtynsky, accessed November 1, 2018. www.edwardburtynsky.com/projects/photographs /water.
2. Marie Watt, "Blanket Stories: Western Door, Salt Sacks and Three Sisters," Rockwell Museum, accessed November 1, 2018, https://rockwellmuseum .org/exhibits-collections/current-exhibitions/blanket-stories-2017.
3. Ibid.
4. "In Conversation with Marie Watt: A New Coyote Tale," *Art Journal* online, last modified October 19, 2017, http://artjournal.collegeart.org/?p=9492.
5. "Seeing Double: Nick Cave," *Interview* online, last modified September 1, 2011, www.interviewmagazine.com/art/nick-cave-mary-boone-jack -shainman.
6. Katherine Brooks, "Stunning 'Soundsuits' Address the Realities of Racial Profiling in America," *Huffington Post*, last modified October 7, 2016,

www.huffingtonpost.com/entry/nick-cave-soundsuits_us_57f79d
cae4b0e655 eab37e67.

7. "Contemporary Conversations with Nick Cave," Art in Embassies online,
last modified June 16, 2017, www.youtube.com/watch?v=HciYn5htOLU.

8. David Usborne, "Sculpture of 9/11 Victim Removed," *Independent* (UK)
online, last modified September 21, 2002, www.independent.co.uk/news
/world/americas/sculpture-of-911-victim-removed-177596.html.

9. "Eric Fischl Discussing Tumbling Woman at the National Gallery of Canada," Chase Art, Vimeo, https://vimeo.com/141074447.

Chapter 9: Grace Will Lead Us Home

1. Carlo McCormick, "Kiki Smith," *Journal of Contemporary Art* 4, no. 1
(1991): 81–95, www.jca-online.com/ksmith.html.

Appendix: Heyman Honey Cake

1. B'nai Shalom Sisterhood, *A Matzo Ball Is Not Another Dress-Up Dance!* (Wa-
verly, IA: G&R, 1983).

Photography Credits

Page 46   Lornado in the winter: Courtesy of Couvrette/Ottawa

Page 49   The staff of Lornado: Courtesy of Vicki Heyman

Page 52   Vicki with the Lornado sign: Courtesy of Gillian
                 Catrambone

Page 62   Bruce and Vicki at Tim Hortons: Courtesy of Gillian
                 Catrambone

Page 64   Bruce with Bob as Santa: Courtesy of Vicki Heyman

Page 70   Bruce with Ray's RCMP hat: Courtesy of Vicki Heyman

Page 73   Bruce and Vicki with Prime Minister Stephen Harper and
                 Laureen Harper in the Prime Minister's Office: Courtesy of
                 Deb Ransom

Page 78   A key on a stone: Courtesy of Vicki Heyman

Page 83   Heyman Hot Sauce from Ola Cocina: Courtesy of Vicki
                 Heyman

Page 86   The garden at Lornado: Courtesy of Vicki Heyman

Page 88   Vicki gardening with local schoolchildren: Courtesy of U.S.
                 Embassy Ottawa/Public Domain

Page 93   Vicki's great-grandmother Tybae Simons: Courtesy of Vicki
                 Heyman

Page 96   Bruce with Johnny and the Colville Bay sign: Courtesy of
                 Vicki Heyman

Page 97   Sourtoe Cocktail: Courtesy of Bruce Heyman

Page 101 (*top*):   Eileen Jacobson and her smoked fish: Courtesy of Vicki
                 Heyman

Page 101 (*bottom*): The community freezer in Tuktoyaktuk: Courtesy of Vicki
                 Heyman

Page 107   Vicki touching the Arctic waters: Courtesy of Bruce
                 Heyman

Page 112   Bruce with Prime Minister Justin Trudeau: Courtesy of Adam
                 Scotti, Office of the Prime Minister

Page 119   Bruce with Ken Taylor: Courtesy of Vicki Heyman

Page 131   Marie Watt's blanket tower: Courtesy of Couvrette/Ottawa

Page 133   Marie Watt's sewing circle at the National Gallery of Canada:
                 Courtesy of Andrea Cordonier

Page 200   President Obama enters Parliament: Courtesy of Vicki Heyman

Page 205   Prime Minister Justin Trudeau hugs Vicki: Courtesy of Farah Mohamed

Page 215   Bruce speaking on election night: Courtesy of Vicki Heyman

Page 222   The Trudeau children with Prime Minister Justin and Sophie, learning to bake cookies: Courtesy of Bruce Heyman

Page 225   Vicki dancing with Roger: Courtesy of Ashley Fraser Photography

Page 227   Lornado staff at Lornado's entrance: Courtesy of Bruce Heyman

Page 230   Starfish in Peggy's Cove: Courtesy of Vicki Heyman

Page 235   A sign at the Women's March: Courtesy of Vicki Heyman

Page 239   "Yes we can" at the Women's March: Courtesy of Vicki Heyman

Insert

Page 1 (*top*)   Bruce and Vicki at their Vanderbilt University graduation: Courtesy of the Heyman family

Page 1 (*bottom*)   Bruce and Vicki at Wrigley Field: Courtesy of Gillian Catrambone

Page 2 (*top*)   Senator Barack Obama and Michelle Obama: Courtesy of Jeanne Rogers

Page 2 (*bottom*)   Bruce and Vicki with their daughter Caroline and President Obama at his Hyde Park home: Courtesy of Obama campaign staff

Page 3   Election night 2012 celebration: Courtesy of Vicki Heyman

Page 4 (*top*)   Bruce, Vicki, and family at the swearing-in with Vice President Joe Biden: Courtesy of U.S. Embassy Ottawa/Public Domain and Jeanne Rogers

Page 4 (*bottom*)   Vicki in front of Rideau Hall: Courtesy of Bruce Heyman

Page 5   Bruce and Vicki meet Prime Minister Stephen Harper: Courtesy of Deb Ransom

Page 6 (*top*)   Bruce and Vicki entering the National Gallery of Canada: Courtesy of Canada 2020

Page 6 (*bottom*)   Bruce and Vicki with Prime Minister Justin Trudeau and Sophie Grégoire Trudeau: Courtesy of Adam Scotti, Office of the Prime Minister

Page 7 (*top*)   Vicki welcoming a Mountie: Courtesy of Ashley Fraser Photography

Page 7 (*bottom*)   Bruce and Vicki in the library at Lornado: Courtesy of David D. Pistol "The Soulful Architect"

Page 8 (*top*)   Bruce and Vicki hosting a salon at Lornado: Courtesy of U.S. Embassy Ottawa/Public Domain

Page 8 (*bottom*)   Bruce and Prime Minister Justin Trudeau laughing together: Courtesy of Adam Scotti, Office of the Prime Minister

Page 9   Bruce and his grandfather's army uniform: Courtesy of Vicki Heyman

Page 10 (*top left*)   Lornado garden: Courtesy of U.S. Embassy Ottawa/Public Domain

Page 10 (*top right*)   Bruce trying a BeaverTail: Courtesy of Vicki Heyman

Page 10 (*bottom left*) Heyman family July Fourth party: Courtesy of Ashley Fraser Photography

Page 10 (*bottom right*) Vicki with Madame Donna Chevrier of Ola Cocina: Courtesy of Bruce Heyman

Page 11 (*top*)   *Tumbling Woman* in the embassy: Courtesy of U.S. Embassy Ottawa/Public Domain

Page 11 (*bottom*)   Bruce and Vicki with watercolor *Tumbling Woman*: Courtesy of Couvrette/Ottawa

Page 12 (*top*)   Michaëlle Jean, Bruce and Vicki dancing: Courtesy of Chris Roussakis

Page 12 (*center*)   Bruce and Vicki learn bee farming: Courtesy of Ted Norris

Page 12 (*bottom*)   Remembrance Day—Bruce and Prime Minister Trudeau: Courtesy of Adam Scotti, Office of the Prime Minister

Page 13 (*top*)   Bruce speaking with President Obama in the Oval Office: Courtesy of Pete Souza/The White House

Page 13 (*bottom*)   Vicki with Sophie Grégoire Trudeau: Courtesy of Bruce Heyman

Page 14 (*top*)   Vicki views Carlos Amorales's art installation at The Power Plant in Toronto: Courtesy of U.S. Consulate General Toronto/Public Domain

Page 14 (*bottom*) July Fourth party/dancing with grandchildren: Courtesy of Ashley Fraser Photography

Page 15 (*top*)   Laughter during President Obama's visit to Parliament: Courtesy of Adam Scotti, Office of the Prime Minister

Page 15 (*bottom*) Bruce and Prime Minister Justin Trudeau embrace: Courtesy of Adam Scotti, Office of the Prime Minister

Page 16   Canada 150 celebration: Courtesy of Stephen Wilkes; *Canada 150*, Ottawa, from the "Day to Night" series, 2017

Index

NOTE: Italic page numbers refer to picture captions.

About the Authors

AVENNE CALGARY, SHELLEY ARNUSCH

AMBASSADOR BRUCE HEYMAN served as the United States ambassador to Canada under President Barack Obama from 2014 until 2017. Currently, Bruce serves as a strategic advisor to Canada 2020, a Canadian progressive think tank based in Ottawa. Also, he serves as co-chair of the Woodrow Wilson Center's Canada Institute Advisory Board. He appears regularly on CBC, CNBC, Fox Business, Bloomberg, CTV, and other media outlets as an expert on trade and bilateral issues. He lives in Chicago with his wife and co-author, Vicki Heyman.

Connect with Bruce on Twitter **@BruceAHeyman**.

VICKI HEYMAN is on the board of the Council for Canadian American Relations, Chicago Media Project, and the international advisory board of C2 Montréal. Vicki served as an American cultural envoy in Canada, leading cross-border conversations and programs related to the arts, social innovation, and youth engagement. Vicki lives in Chicago where she and Bruce are co-founders of Uncharted, LLC.

Connect with Vicki on Twitter **@vshey**.

Please visit the Heymans at **artofdiplomacybook.com**.